The Economics of Prohibition

The Economics of Prohibition

Mark Thornton

University of Utah Press
Salt Lake City

∞ The paper in this book meets the standards for
permanence and durability established by the
Committee on Production Guidelines for Book Longevity
of the Council on Library Resources

Library of Congress Cataloging-in-Publication Data

Thornton, Mark.
    The economics of prohibition / Mark Thornton.
        p.   cm.
    Includes bibliographical references and index.
    ISBN 0–87480–375–6 (alk. paper). — ISBN 0–87480–379–9 (pbk. :
alk. paper)
    1. Prohibition—Economic aspects. 2. Prohibition—Economic
aspects—United States. 3. Narcotics, Control of—Economic aspects—
United States. 4. Drug traffic—Economic aspects—United States.
5. Narcotics and crime—Economic aspects—United States. I. Title.
HV5088.T48 1991
338.4'336341'0973—dc20   91–50333
                                                                            CIP

Contents

Foreword

Foreign wars come and go, but the Drug War is a constant of U.S. domestic policy. For nearly eight decades the government has attempted to prevent American citizens from using one or more illicit substances. By the 1980s the government's efforts had become truly draconian: more than one million drug arrests annually; minimum drug sentences that exceed the average punishment for murderers and rapists; increasing numbers of wiretaps; property confiscations and home evictions based on mere suspicion of drug use; ever more warrantless searches as part of the constantly expanding "drug exception" to the Fourth Amendment; growing involvement of the Central Intelligence Agency, Department of Defense, and National Guard; citywide curfews; and proposals for everything from shooting down unidentified planes at the border to declaring martial law.

Yet these efforts have yielded few positive results. The U.S. now has more than one million people in prison, yielding the highest rate of imprisonment in the industrial world. Young blacks are more likely to die in gun battles in the criminal underground, funded by drug prohibition, than they were while serving in the army in Vietnam. Drug users seeking to pay the inflated prices of illegal substances commit thousands of property crimes in cities and their suburbs. Children, who receive lesser criminal punishments, are increasingly recruited into the drug trade, where many become users.

Moreover, the law appears to have stopped few people from trying illicit substances. According to the National Institute on Drug Abuse, 74.4 million people over the age of 12 have tried drugs, despite decades of drug prohibition. Nearly 27 million use illegal substances at least once a year. Rates of drug use are now falling, but the declines started before the periodic escalations of the drug war during the 1980s.

Given this record, it is time to fundamentally reevaluate America's drug policy. To do so risks attack from publicity-minded drug czars and vote-seeking politicians. But not to do so acquiesces to a policy that is needlessly imprisoning, maiming, and killing tens of thousands of people for voluntarily using and selling substances that are demonstrably less harmful—particularly in the number of deaths they cause—than the legal drugs alcohol and tobacco, the latter of which is subsidized by the federal government.

Courageously picking up the gauntlet tossed down by the drug war lobby is Mark Thornton. In a debate more often marked by emotion than facts, Professor Thornton looks at how illegal drug markets, for alcohol as well as today's disfavored substances, really work. Particularly important is his conclusion that such problems as crime and corruption are natural outgrowths of drug prohibition, not drug use. As a result, the deaths of innocent bystanders in drug dealers' gun battles, for example, create an argument for drug legalization, not stricter enforcement.

Many readers may nevertheless disagree with Professor Thornton's conclusions. But they will still have an obligation to respond to his evidence that the costs of prohibition are huge and obvious, while the benefits are few and dubious. The burden of proving Professor Thornton wrong, and thereby justifying continuation of the drug war, now rests on those who oppose drug legalization.

Cato Institute   DOUG BANDOW

Acknowledgments

During my study of prohibition I have been helped by many friends and colleagues. Their encouragement, suggestions, and corrections made this book possible.

My gratitude and respect go to John D. Jackson, who provided the critical guidance so crucial to the completion of this project. The unceasing stream of comments and suggestions from Richard D. Ault and Leland B. Yeager contributed both insights and a broad perspective. Seth A. Anderson provided valuable suggestions and encouraged me in my efforts to find a publisher.

It is to the credit of my teacher, coauthor, colleague, and friend Robert B. Ekelund, Jr., that the lessons and debates in his classroom turned my question into an answer—an answer that forms the foundation of this book.

I owe a special debt to the University of Utah Press, whose staff had the courage and foresight to bring this book to fruition. I am also grateful to the distinguished group of reviewers assembled for this project—Bruce Benson, Charles Maurice, and Murray Rothbard—each of whom provided valuable comments and corrections.

Three institutions have provided support for this project. The Institute for Humane Studies at George Mason University provided my initial exposure to classical liberalism and academic research. I wish to offer my thanks for the 1990 F. Leroy Hill Summer Faculty Fellowship, and I give special thanks to Sheldon Richman for his assistance in preparing this manscript for publication.

I also wish to acknowledge the H. B. Earhart Foundation for its financial assistance during the preparation of this book.

My very special thanks go to the members and staff of the Ludwig von Mises Institute. The intellectual environment, continuous encouragement, and financial support they provided were invaluable. For their assistance and faith in me, I would especially like to thank Llewellyn H. Rockwell and O. P. Alford III.

It is my hope that the publication of this book begins to repay all those who have shown so much confidence in me.

Introduction

Prohibition has an ever-increasing impact on our daily life. In the United States, prohibition against certain drugs, involving "wars" on them, has become one of our most visible and hotly debated national problems. The purpose of the following investigation is to improve our understanding of the origins and results of prohibition, and therefore indirectly to contribute to future policy-making, shifting it toward rationality.

At the core of this book, one of the first theoretical investigations of prohibition, is an economic theory of prohibition, which defines prohibition as a government decree against the exchange of a good or service. Recent studies of decrees against cocaine, heroin, and marijuana suggest that these prohibitions impose heavy costs and are extremely difficult to enforce. Beyond such costs and enforcement difficulties, however, I argue that effective prohibition is impossible to achieve, because the unintended consequences of prohibition itself preclude any benefits.

The only long-term solution to the problems engendered by the "misuse" of a product, I maintain, is legalization of that product. With legalization, as opposed to decriminalization and other forms of government interventionism, the government treats the misused product or service as if it were soybeans, computer chips, or pencils. The market is controlled by self-interest and normal legal constraints, such as product-liability law.

This book may be viewed as a challenge to prohibitionists to present a theory that describes the benefits of prohibition. It may also be seen as a challenge to those who recommend that prohibition be replaced with some form of decriminalization. While it may be a good transition policy, decriminalization (government drugstores, high taxation, high fines, etc.) would maintain a black market, is an unstable policy, and does not create the necessary preconditions for reversing or limiting drug abuse.

I have made use of historical analysis and applications of theory in this book, incorporating the disciplines of economics, history, criminology, sociology, and political science as needed. I have avoided using such items as estimates of elasticity and regression analysis because they are transient, unnecessary, and provide a false sense of certainty.

The historical perspective transforms what might appear to be an implausible position into an eminently sensible one. The important historical aspects I examine include the role of economists in prohibitions, the origins of prohibitions, product quality, crime rates, and political corruption during prohibitions.

There is little doubt about the importance of prohibition in American history and its role in social problems. The prohibition of alcohol sales was a crucial aspect of trade and tension with the indigenous Indian population. Temperance (along with slavery) was the primary reform movement in antebellum America, and prohibition was a determining political issue at the state and local level.

After the Civil War, prohibitionism spread from New England both west and south. Although sometimes perceived as a lull in the drive for prohibition, the period from 1860 to 1900 saw the establishment of the building blocks of successful national prohibitions. Addiction was discovered, the Prohibition party was formed, groups such as the Women's Christian Temperance Union and the Anti-Saloon League were established, and a wave of prohibitions at the state and local level were enacted on alcohol, cocaine, opium, morphine, gambling, and prostitution.

The Progressive Era (1900–1920) marks the pinnacle of American prohibitionism. As America "progressed" to become an imperial power, it did so in part on the international prohibition of narcotics and the Harrison Narcotics Act. The act also helped the medical and drug industries "progress" toward the exalted monopoly status that they now enjoy.

The Progressive Era also witnessed wartime prohibition of alcohol and National Alcohol Prohibition (the Eighteenth Amendment to the U.S. Constitution). Never have so many been deceived about so much by so few. The Eighteenth Amendment and the Volstead Act, which established the mechanism of the amendment's enforcement, would be decisive and negative factors in American life and culture for over a decade.

The failure of Prohibition helped remove it temporarily from public attention. Not only was the "noble experiment" an embarrassment, events such as the Great Depression and World War II dominated public concern. Marijuana prohibition in 1937 was relatively insignificant—a mere side effect of narcotics and alcohol prohibitions.

The current prohibitions against narcotics originated with war and foreign-policy considerations in the Far East. In the 1960s foreign-policy considerations which resulted in war in Vietnam brought about increased consumption of drugs and the ensuing intensified war on drugs.

One early lesson from American history is the unmistakable interaction between war, intemperance, and prohibition. Avoiding war is perhaps the most important thing a government can do to avoid intemperance, addiction, and drug abuse. Conversely, drug abuse and prohibitions are a significant long-term cost of war.

History also supports the finding that prohibition is impossible to achieve in the economic sense. Legislatures do enact prohibitions and establish penalties and enforcement bureaus. The actions of these bureaus to enforce prohibition decrees have an effect, and when a prohibition survives long enough to be enforced it is *successful* in a political sense. I argue, however, that prohibitions have no socially desirable effect.

Of course prohibition should not be evaluated against a higher standard than other laws. Murder is against the law, but not all murderers are apprehended, convicted, and punished. Likewise, to expect complete or perfect prohibition is unrealistic. Rather, prohibition will be measured against its public-spirited intentions, that is, to reduce consumption of a good in order indirectly to reduce social ills (such as crime, destruction of free will, drug-related deaths) and to promote social goals (family life, democracy, health, and economic development).

To the extent that prohibitions result in increased prices, they produce increased crime and political corruption. Higher prices for a prohibited product also result in the substitution of related products and the innovation of more dangerous substitutes. Prohibited products tend to be more dangerous than legal substitutes in many respects, the result of prohibition, not the product itself. Therefore, to assume that more severe penalties or increased enforcement will result in the substitution of legal for prohibited products is to make an invalid conclusion. Prohibitions on drugs cause potency to increase. Therefore, the assumption that higher prices achieve the goals of prohibition is unfounded. Given all such considerations, the case for prohibition remains unfounded even if the indirect connection between the consumption of certain products and social ills does exist.

The attempt to understand all human action (as opposed to just commercial activity) as rational represents a revolution in thought. Applied to policy decisions, this revolution is called public–choice economics, and from this perspective it is unacceptable to present prohibition as an ignorant, irrational, or impossible social policy.

Economists now suspect that any net losses to society produced by government policies are the result of *rent seeking* rather than ignorance or irrationality on the part of policymakers. Rent seeking is a search for privilege and personal gain through the political process. *Rent seeking* is distinguished from *corruption* in that rent seeking is legal and corruption is not.

History reveals that prohibitions are indeed classic examples of the co-opting of public-spirited intentions by rent seekers within the political process, thereby explaining the existence of what at first appears to be irrational policies.

This rationality-based method for the study of human action was labeled praxeology by the Austrian economist Ludwig von Mises. His student F. A. Hayek, a Nobel laureate, called it the logic of choice. Contemporary economists will recognize this approach as developed by Gary Becker. Other social scientists, notably political scientists, criminologists, and psychologists, will no doubt recognize this rationality-based approach as one which has become part of their own disciplines.

Although such an outcome is unintentional on my part, this book will prove threatening to many. Some will label the theory in it doctrinaire, apologetic, capitalistic, or liberal. Specialists may find it lacking for neglecting the role of addiction or for failing to consider certain estimates of elasticity, particular chemical compositions, or the role that unusual circumstances have played in particular markets at points in time.

In fact, however, many of the problems that economists and other social scientists have had with prohibition is that they have proceeded with investigation of specific markets without the benefit of a general theory.

One last warning is in order, and it cannot be emphasized enough. The markets in which prohibition has been deployed, such as gambling, intoxicants, and prostitution, have existed for a long time and will continue long after I and my book turn to dust. Prostitution is the world's oldest profession; people have been using intoxicants for as long as history can record; and men and women are risk-taking, fun-loving creatures. Most human beings live for leisure, not for labor. Labor is merely a means to an end.

No matter how deplorable the above activities appear to some, they are "leisure" to others. The only consistently successful method for raising the standards of leisure to higher levels is to allow economic development to take place. Individuals who use certain products or activities to self-destruct have problems far worse than the visible ones. Prohibition of these goods or services will have little impact in such cases.

It is also important to recognize that the problems in these markets (disease, fraud, broken families, and so on) are not the result of a lack of government involvement. Indeed, these markets have been historically characterized by extensive government involvement prior to the enactment of prohibition.

It is hoped that this book will stimulate debate, in both the academic and policy communities, even among those who disagree with aspects of it, and by that debate move us to a more rational public policy.

1

Economists and Prohibition

I hold that there is nothing much wrong with standard economic methodology as laid down in the first chapter of almost
every textbook in economic theory; what is wrong is that
economists do not practice what they preach.
—Mark Blaug, *The Methodology of Economics*

Since economists have been leading the battle against drug prohibition, most people would be surprised to learn that they played
an important role in establishing and defending the alcohol prohibition of the 1920s. It is still an open question whether economists set
public opinion or mirror it, but the relationship between economists
and prohibition provides interesting insights into the economics profession, the origins of Prohibition, and the current debate over drug
legalization.

In recent years economists have led the fight to legalize—actually,
to *re*legalize—drugs. The Nobel Prize-winning economist Milton
Friedman has been the outspoken leader of the relegalization forces.
His open letter to "Drug Czar" William Bennett, published in the
Wall Street Journal, is just his latest salvo against the prohibitionist
establishment.[1] Friedman began this battle in the 1960s, writing in
Newsweek that the prohibition of drugs was ineffective and that more
reasonable and prudent approaches to the problems of drug abuse
were available. He (with his wife, Rose Friedman) later attacked drug
prohibition in *Free to Choose* and *The Tyranny of the Status Quo*, linking
the harm it causes with the experience of alcohol prohibition in the

---

[1]See Friedman 1989.

1920s. The Friedmans are careful observers of history who oppose drug prohibition both on ethical and practical grounds.

One of Friedman's former colleagues at the University of Chicago, Gary S. Becker (1987), has also come out strongly against drug prohibition in the popular media. His support for the relegalization of drugs is significant because of his status in the profession, and for his potential as a Nobel Prize winner in economics. Becker argues that prohibition is not working and that the costs far outweigh the benefits. He bases his position both on current findings and on his own theoretical research. Becker is the foremost current authority and advocate of the rationality assumption regarding the study of human behavior. Among his numerous articles on the economics of human behavior is his recently published "A Theory of Rational Addiction" (with Kevin Murphy), in which addiction is modeled as rational behavior.

Another important economist to announce support for legalization is the former secretary of state George Shultz. Since Shultz was a key member of the Reagan administration, his public statement is a major development in the debate over drug policy. The pro-legalization position of William F. Buckley, Jr., and Shultz's conversion to legalization mark a major turning point in conservative thought.

A survey of economists indicates that the majority oppose prohibition and favor moving policy in the direction of decriminalization. Economists who specialize in monetary theory and public finance are more likely to support decriminalization, while specialists in business administration are more apt to defend prohibition. Economists who work in the private sector generally support decriminalization, whereas government economists are more likely to support prohibition. It should be noted that economists overwhelmingly fall within the demographic grouping that exhibits the most support for legalization within the general public (middle aged, male, highly educated, upper income, Jewish or nonreligious). Most graduates of the top graduate programs and most economists trained in the Chicago, public choice, or Austrian traditions supported decriminalization of illegal drugs (Thornton 1991).

The growing importance of and interest in prohibition has led some economists to include discussions of laws against alcohol, drugs, gambling, and pornography in their textbooks. Normally restrained and politically neutral, several writers of economic textbooks have taken a skeptical view of all prohibitions. For example, when examining the current drug prohibition, Edwin G. Dolan and John C. Goodman (1989, 35) present "misgivings raised on grounds of efficiency, equality, and liberty." Robert B. Ekelund and Robert D. Tollison (1988, 108) find that "(e)conomic analysis casts doubts on the effects of directing increased resources into enforcement without careful analysis of the probable consequences of such programs," and they suggest "that government expenditures would be better directed to the demand side of the problem."[2]

Richard McKenzie and Gordon Tullock (1989), too, place a warning label on prohibition. They find that "the costs of enforcement should, perhaps, be taken into account now in evaluating the efficacy of contemporary laws against hard drugs or pornography" (7). McKenzie and Tullock also assert that economists have always been in agreement against prohibition and have been aware of the tremendous costs, as if alerted by some standard economic model: "If backers of prohibition had consulted economists, *we are sure* they would have been told that the law would be very difficult and expensive to enforce. With this advice they might have decided not to undertake the program of moral elevation" (7; emphasis added).

It is true that economists were in substantial agreement during the formative years of national alcohol prohibition. But they were for it— not against it.

THE ORIGINS OF THE "ECONOMICS" OF PROHIBITION

Economists helped establish the case for prohibition during the Progressive Era, a time when they were professionalizing their discipline and when a movement toward government interventionism and socialism, promoted by the German Historical School, was displacing the classical liberal approach to political economy. Members of the German Historical School rejected economic theory in favor of the study of history and institutions. Derived from German romantic philosophy (Hegelian determinism) the School advocated the use of laws as a means to social reform.

Graduates of the German Historical School, principally Richard

[2]Ekelund and Tollison's conclusions are based in part on Thornton 1986, an earlier version of chapter 4 of this book.

T. Ely, founded the American Economic Association in 1890. The association was modeled after German academic associations that allied themselves with the German state. Many market-oriented economists threatened to boycott the new organization because of its outwardly political bias. Once its socialistic statement of principle was dropped, however, the association became widely accepted.

Many of the founding members were raised in puritanical households of postmillennialist pietism.[3] During their days as university students many became atheists, substituting a secular approach to perfectionism for the religious approach of their parents. Some, such as Richard T. Ely, adopted a prosocialist orientation, while others, such as John Bates Clark, adopted a "dog-eat-dog" evolutionary perspective on capitalism. What they shared was an evangelical outlook and a strong dislike of such products as alcohol.[4]

One of the founding members of the association and a leading proponent of prohibition was Simon N. Patten. Patten was a misfit. Handicapped by poor health and eyesight, he was unsuited for traditional pursuits and was considered the oddball of his prosperous family. Born into a traditional Yankee puritan home, Patten became an intellectual and agnostic. After several setbacks in his life he went to Germany, where he was trained by a leader of the German Historical School, Karl Knies. Upon returning to America he could not find a job until he was hired by fellow supporters of protectionism and friends at the Wharton School of the University of Pennsylvania.

A. W. Coats (1987) describes Patten as original and idiosyncratic, his publications unusual and eccentric. Patten's contributions "were

---

[3]Postmillennial pietists believe that there will be a thousand-year kingdom of God on earth and that it is man's responsibility to establish the necessary conditions as a prerequisite for Jesus' return.

[4]In a sobering passage, Newcomb (1886, 11–13) used the drinking of alcohol (i.e., "gratifying the morbid appetite") to distinguish correctly between the sphere of moralists and the role of political economists—to separate "the totally different . . . questions whether an end is good and how an end can best be attained." Newcomb suggests that the "economist might say in conclusion" that he knows "of no way in which a man can be made to accept that which he desires less in preference to that which he desires more, except positive restraint."

intriguing but puzzlingly novel and unsystematic, yet his awareness of the costs of growth and his concern for the environment anticipated late 20th century anxieties" (818–19). Despite extensive writings and his role as a founder (and later president) of the American Economic Association, Patten is remembered not for his theories but for his "prophecies."

One such prophecy was the advent of alcohol prohibition in America. Patten was a pluralist, believing that a policy is neither all good nor all bad and that a policy may very well be good for one country but disastrous for another. He wrote in 1890 that alcohol prohibition was a good policy for America and that abstinence would be the inevitable result of evolutionary competition.

Prohibition was both desirable and inevitable in America from Patten's evolutionary perspective. Patten based his conclusion on three main factors: (1) severe weather variation in America results in heavy and irregular alcohol consumption; (2) the custom of "treating" in America results in people consuming a greater quantity and variety of alcoholic drinks than if they relied solely on their own decisions; (3) technological advance resulted in the production of higher-potency and lower-quality alcoholic beverages. All three of these conditions were relative to conditions in Germany, where Patten was trained and where prohibition was apparently unnecessary.

Patten seems to argue that prohibition must be adopted if we are to "survive." Temperate people will "outcompete" heavy-drinking societies in terms of longevity, prodigy, and wealth. Temperate societies will overcome the intemperate because a given amount of land can support two temperate people or one heavy drinker. America will decline as the soil is exhausted in an attempt to support a nation of drunkards. For Patten, prohibition is a great evolutionary battleground because America must go dry if it is to survive and prosper: "Separate out the good in society from the bad, and you take from the bad many of the restraints which keep them from crime. In this way every measure that makes the good better makes the bad worse. The sharper the lines are drawn between the two classes, the more will the good progress and the quicker will the bad run through their downward course. With prohibition it is easier to be good and more dangerous to be bad" (1890, 65).

For Patten, alcohol is a product with no equilibrium in consumption. One is either good and abstains from alcohol, or one becomes a drunkard and self-destructs. Patten even presented an early version of the escalating drug-use theory (that is, marijuana use leads to heroin addiction) when he referred to

that graded series of drinks found in every saloon by which the drinker passes gradually to stronger drinks as weaker ones lose their attraction. This tendency divides society into two parts, and forces the respectable to join in a compact opposition to all drinking. The sharper this contest becomes the more have the abstainers to gain. Little by little will their economic advantage increase their strength, until their moral influence will keep the drinker from the saloon and their political power will take the saloon from the drinker. (1890, 67–68)

Patten links virtually all the problems of modern society (real and imagined) with drunkenness. His obsession with drunkenness is indicated by his somewhat confusing concluding statement of his first English publication:

The increase of drunkenness and other physical vices which have accompanied modern progress are the result of the extended division of labor, which destroys the ability both to produce and to enjoy most of those things that are sources of pleasure to man in an isolated state. We can obtain the advantage derived from the division of labor without losing the ability to enjoy all kinds of produce only by so educating all the faculties of man that he will have that independence and all those sources of pleasure which isolated men enjoy. Moreover, those qualities which increase the sources of pleasure are the very ones by which the field of employment is enlarged and the tendency to overpopulate is reduced, and only when education has developed all the qualities in every man can we expect this tendency to become so harmless that all men can enjoy the pleasures of an isolated state along with the efficiency of modern civilization. The End. ([1885] 1968, 244)

On this argument, Patten formed the economic rationale for prohibition and helped set the alcohol agenda of American economists. Like William Graham Sumner and John Bates Clark, he perceived that survival of the fittest would eventually eliminate the drunkard from society. The interventionist bias in his education, however, propelled Patten to conclude that prohibition combined with evolutionary competition would achieve the desired results (total abstinence) much quicker than evolution alone.[5]

IN DEFENSE OF PROHIBITION

An important American economist, Irving Fisher, was the champion of Prohibition within the profession. He organized a round-table discussion on the topic at the American Economic Association meetings in 1927. Here he claimed to have been unable to find even one economist to speak against Prohibition, despite a thorough search.

I got a list of the economists who are supposed to be opposed to Prohibition, and wrote to them; they all replied either that I was mistaken in thinking that they were opposed to Prohibition or that, if we were going to confine the discussion to the economics of Prohibition, they would not care to respond. When I found that I was to have no speaker representing the opposite point of view, I wrote to all American economists listed in "Minerva" and all American teachers of statistics. I have not received from any one an acceptance. (I. Fisher et al. 1927, 5)

Contrary to the belief of McKenzie and Tullock, if the supporters of alcohol prohibition had asked economists about it, they would have been heartily encouraged.

In 1926 Fisher conveyed an optimistic, almost utopian view toward the elimination of the poisonous drink and the problems often associated with alcohol consumption. The 1920s was a time of great optimism, and Fisher best described the optimism concerning Prohibition:

Prohibition is here to stay. If not enforced, its blessings will speedily turn into a curse. There is no time to lose. Although things are much better than before Prohibition, with the possible exception of disrespect for law, they may not stay so. Enforcement will cure disrespect

---

[5]Boswell 1934, 48; also see Fox 1967, 104–5. Most American economists of this time took a dim view of alcohol use. It is interesting to note that Veblen built his concept of "conspicuous consumption" partly on the basis of goods such as alcohol, tobacco, and narcotics.

for law and other evils complained of, as well as greatly augment the good. American Prohibition will then go down in history as ushering in a new era in the world, in which accomplishment this nation will take pride forever. (I. Fisher [1926] 1927, 239)

Fisher's staunch support of Prohibition helped to insulate the policy from criticism. He wrote three books on Prohibition in which his academic status and objectivity thinly cloaked his avid support.[6] He promoted the claims that Prohibition would reduce crime, improve the moral fabric of society, and increase productivity and the standard of living. Indeed, he maintained that Prohibition was partly responsible for the economic prosperity of the Roaring Twenties.

Fisher, a genius in many respects, was born into a Protestant family of Puritan stock. His father was a preacher and a graduate of Yale Divinity School, and his mother was at least as zealous as his father. The death of his father and two older siblings, as well as his own poor health, had a major impact on his views concerning social policy. He supported anything, such as Prohibition, that *might* extend life expectancy.

Fisher's atheism would appear to place him at odds with religious reformers, the principal supporters of Prohibition. Still, though Fisher gave up belief in God and religion, he remained convinced of the doctrines and methods of postmillennialist evangelical Protestantism. Men should work toward the goals of morality, progress, and order while on this earth, he believed, and government should be the main instrument of civilization. Method was secondary to achieving desirable ends. This outlook would typify his work in economics and social policy. "Men cannot enjoy the benefits of civilized liberty without restrictions. Law and Order must prevail, else confusion takes their place, and, with the coming of Confusion, Freedom vanishes" (quoted in I. N. Fisher 1956, 13).

Fisher was most adept at mathematics and helped support himself through scholarships, academic contests, and tutoring. His dissertation was an exercise in a mathematical-theoretical reconstruc-

---

[6]Fisher's main contributions to the study of Prohibition include those published in [1926] 1927, and 1930. A biography of Fisher by his son, Irving Norton Fisher (1956), details Fisher's activist approach to social problems.

tion of utility theory that drew heavily on the method of Léon Walras.

The thesis was applauded by Francis Yisdro Edgeworth, who repudiated aspects of his own theory after reading Fisher's work. Vilfredo Pareto wrote Fisher an eight-page letter in which he spoke scornfully of the "adversaries of mathematical methods," and praised Fisher's distinction between utility of "that which cannot be useful, and that which is really useful."[7] It was this distinction that Fisher used later in the analysis of alcohol consumption.

To admirers of Fisher's more scientific contributions, he appears eminently scientific and objective. His work on Prohibition reveals a thin layer of scientific veneer that is important for evaluating all his contributions, for Fisher was clearly an advocate of government intervention in the economy. A key insight into his viewpoint is illustrated by an excerpt from his speech to the Yale Socialist Club in November 1941.[8]

I believe [William Graham Sumner] was one of the greatest professors we ever had at Yale, but I have drawn far away from his point of view, that of the old laissez faire doctrine.

I remember he said in his classroom: "Gentlemen, the time is coming when there will be two great classes, Socialists, and Anarchists. The Anarchists want the government to be nothing, and the Socialists want government to be everything. There can be no greater contrast. Well, the time will come when there will be only these two great parties, the Anarchists representing the laissez faire doctrine and the Socialists representing the extreme view on the other side, and when that time comes I am an Anarchist."

That amused his class very much, for he was as far from a revolutionary as you could expect. But I would like to say that if that time comes when there are two great parties, Anarchists and Socialists, then I am a Socialist. (Quoted in I. N. Fisher 1956, 44)

Fisher's initial position on alcohol problems was that education of the youth was the best solution. Alcohol had its grip on drinkers, just as opium had its grip on dope fiends. The older generations

---

[7]The attention received for this distinction is described in Fisher's biography (I. N. Fisher 1956, 48–50). Edgeworth's review of Fisher's dissertation appeared in the March 1893 issue of *Economic Journal*.

[8]For further illustration of Irving Fisher as a technocratic-type socialist, see his presidential address to the American Economic Association in 1919.

would have to be forgotten, with all efforts concentrated on the youth. In an address to the students of Oberlin College in the spring of 1912, he summarized his position on intoxicants: "But what is the normal use of these things (beer, whiskey, opium, hashish, and tobacco)? According to the best light scientifically that has been shed on them, the normal use is none at all, and if that is so those who see it should not be ashamed to live up to their ideal any more than they should be ashamed to live up to the Ten Commandments" (quoted in I. N. Fisher 1956, 152–53). In testimony before the Subcommittee on Excise and Liquor Legislation for the District of Columbia (1912) he stated: "After making what I believe was a thoroughly disinterested study of the question, . . . I came personally very strongly to the conclusion, on the basis of statistics as well as on the basis of physiology that alcohol so far as we can observe its effects, is an evil and no benefit" (quoted in I. N. Fisher 1956, 153–54). Later he became convinced that antisaloon legislation would be necessary to supplement education efforts, and he was converted to prohibition by the "success" of state prohibitions.

During World War I, Fisher volunteered his services to the Council on National Defense, where he was assigned the task of establishing wartime policy on alcohol. Under his direction the council recommended wartime prohibition and dry zones around all army cantonments. The alcohol interests blocked the first measure, which Fisher supported because he considered the war an excellent opportunity to experiment with prohibition. Fisher also surmised that this defeat provided the necessary impetus to bring about prohibition in 1920.[9]

It was as an indirect result of this second defeat of War-time Prohibition that Constitutional Prohibition came about! The brewers found that, unwittingly, they had jumped out of the frying pan into the fire!

The reason was that the Senators who had acceded to President Wilson's request to withdraw the War-time Prohibition clauses from

---

[9]Fisher himself considered the adoption of the Prohibition Amendment a premature act. He felt that more time was needed to establish a national consensus and to provide for education and policy development. Fisher often praised the indirect benefits of World War I, such as the collection of statistics by the federal government, the passage of Prohibition, the opportunity to study inflation, and the powerful jobs made available to economists. See I. N. Fisher 1956, 154; I. Fisher 1918 and 1919; and Rothbard 1989, 115.

the Food Act thereby so disappointed and angered their dry constituents that these Senators felt constrained to do something to set themselves right. (I. Fisher 1927, 10–12)

Fisher's books on Prohibition are empirical examinations of social statistics such as alcohol consumption, criminal activity, and health. In his first book, *Prohibition at Its Worst* (1927), Fisher spoke for himself and was the most confrontational. In *Prohibition Still at Its Worst* (1928) and *The "Noble Experiment"* (1930), he replaced this style with a seemingly more balanced approach in which he presented both "wet" and "dry" views on various issues and empirical points.

In the first book, Fisher laid out his assumptions, or "great facts" which constituted his general plan of analysis. He purported to show that Prohibition was imperfectly enforced, that its results were not as bad as reported, and that it had in fact accomplished much good. He found the personal-liberty argument against Prohibition an *illusion*. Further, he argued that the Volstead Act could not be amended without violating the Eighteenth Amendment, that the Eighteenth Amendment could not be repealed, and that its nullification would be the worst possible disrespect of the law. Finally, he asserted that the "*only* practical solution is to enforce the law" ([1926] 1927, 18–19).

Much of Fisher's work involves disputes over statistics. Still, he can be credited to a large extent with developing the major issues concerning prohibition, organizing the debate between wets and drys, and establishing the criteria by which future prohibitions would be judged. A detailed examination of Fisher's work on prohibition would take a book-length treatment in itself. A critique of some of Fisher's conclusions and suggestions, however, provides a sampling of his shortcomings.

Fisher apologized in later writings for failing to recognize the merits of private prohibition. Before the turn of the century, employers commonly supplied employees with alcohol rations on the job. After 1900, most manufacturers, with their complex and dangerous production processes, did away with alcohol rations, often replacing them with rules against drinking. These changes occurred at a time when courts and state legislatures were increasingly holding employers responsible for injuries to employees.

Fisher seemed puzzled by the distinction between public and private prohibition and by "wet" support for private prohibition but not for that decreed by the government. The fact that changes in the economy made private prohibition economical for some employers seems lost on him. He later admitted that private prohibitions were more effective than the law. "Largely because of the penalties of the workmen's compensation and employers' liability laws, and from considerations of output requirements, the situation has brought about a more absolute form of Prohibition, privately enforced, than that embodied in the Eighteenth Amendment or the Volstead Act" (I. Fisher 1930, 443). This not only indicates that Fisher was in part blind to the market process, it also undermines the empirical analysis throughout his work and that of others. The desirable results of private prohibition and employment policy cannot be attributed to Prohibition.

Fisher felt that public opinion was firmly behind Prohibition because of the increased mechanization in society. He contended that machinery and automobiles could not be safely used after one consumed alcohol. This argument, however, is no better than arguing for a prohibition of cars without considering the costs involved and alternative solutions. Fisher also argued that other systems, such as the ones adopted in Canada (government dispensary) and Great Britain (taxation and regulation), were worse, or at least no better, than Prohibition. Here he was comparing his perceptions of what foreign systems were like in practice with his perception of what American Prohibition would be like if it were "properly enforced."

Fisher argued that consumption of alcohol declined during Prohibition, and several estimates support the view that alcohol consumption per capita did decline. Still, many important questions—how much did consumption decline? what were all the causes for this decline? how did individual consumption patterns change? what type of alcohol was consumed? and what happened to consumption of substitutes?—remained largely unanswered and even unasked. He also contended that the decrease in alcohol consumption fostered economic progress. Although the claim that Prohibition had caused the economic prosperity of the 1920s was discarded with the onset of the Great Depression, his beliefs concerning industrial productivity and absenteeism are still used to inflate estimates of the economic losses from drug use and the potential benefits of prohibition.

In discussing the substitutes for alcohol, Fisher focused on the automobile, radio, and motion-picture industries. In a passage that reads more like a sermon than a tract on economics, he noted that the increased specialization in the economy (apparently also a contribution of Prohibition) allowed for the relief of misery. He considered all substitutes for alcohol as good, and he completely ignored the fact that such substitutes generally resulted in less value for the consumer and might result in a type of substitute that Fisher himself would lament. According to the limited references to narcotics in his writings, Fisher apparently thought that Prohibition had reduced the sale of narcotics and that they might not be as damaging as alcohol.

Fisher felt that Prohibition had worked better than could be expected "hygienically, economically, and socially." The main problem was that it was poorly enforced, particularly in the big cities. He claimed that Prohibition worked where it was properly enforced. Fisher supported a complete reorganization of enforcement at all levels, the hiring of better enforcement officials, and large increases in expenditures on enforcement.

In his final contribution on Prohibition (1930), Fisher uncharacteristically compromised with the wets by supporting the "right" to home production and consumption. He claimed that legalizing home production would reduce the requirements on law enforcement and eliminate the personal-liberty argument from the public debate. It is unclear whether Fisher used this as a last-ditch effort to save Prohibition or if he realized its futility. He admitted that such a modification would decrease the number of opponents of Prohibition by "thousands, if not millions" and would allow law enforcement to concentrate on bootleggers without compromising the closure of saloons. He also made *one* statement admitting the infeasibility of prohibition: "Yet, it is absurd to expect home production to be prevented by enforcement officers" (1930, 454). Both the admission of the infeasibility and the compromise are unique statements from Fisher, and they appear only on the last page of his last book on Prohibition.[10]

Fisher's methodology was poorly suited to a proper assessment

---

[10]By 1933 Fisher must have been thoroughly disheartened with the course of events. A new age of prohibition and scientific management of the economy—a permanent prosperity—had come crashing down around him. Not only had Prohibition been repealed and the economy devastated by the Great Depression, he had lost his personal fortune on his own advice in the stock

of prohibition, particularly when combined with his religious-like zeal to eliminate the use of alcohol and to increase life expectancy. In theoretical matters, Fisher began with the distinction between desires (demand) and attainment of actual satisfaction. His personal impatience, his concern over mortality, and his interest in eugenics and genetic engineering may have contributed to his distinction between desire and attainment of value.

One of the points which I look back upon with satisfaction is that I repudiated the idea of [William Stanley] Jevons that economics was concerned with a "calculus of pleasure and pain" and I insisted there was a great distinction between desires and their satisfactions and that economics had to do only with desires, so far as the influence of market prices was concerned.

But one should be more interested in truth than in who desires the credit for first reaching it. Ever since my six years of illness I have become much more interested in promoting the truth than in claiming credit or even in adding to knowledge. There is so much knowledge already attained that is not yet applied that I have often set myself to work to bring that knowledge to the attention of others.

Today I would like to see a study, partly economic and partly psychological, showing how the human animal following his desires often misses satisfactions instead of attaining them. The star example is narcotics. (Quoted in I. N. Fisher 1956, 339)

No matter how real or important the distinction between desire and attainment of satisfaction is, economists such as Joseph Schumpeter have found that in Fisher's case "the scholar was misled by the crusader." Or as G. Findly Shirras noted, "The drawback to a completely rational mind is that it is very apt to assume that what is flawless in logic is therefore practicable" (quoted in I. N. Fisher 1956, 193–94).

Fisher was much more apt to rely on "facts" and available statistics than on the logic of cause and effect. In the preface to *The Making of Index Numbers*, he illustrated his reliance on statistics and the inductive method by noting: "The present book had its origin in the desire to put these deductive conclusions to an inductive test by means of calculations from actual historical data. But before I had

market. With respect to alcohol he turned his attention to the temperance movement by publishing three editions of a book on the evils of alcohol consumption.

gone far in such testing of my original conclusions, I found to my surprise, that the results of actual calculations constantly suggested further deduction until, in the end, I had completely revised both my conclusions and my theoretical foundations" (quoted in I. N. Fisher 1956, 194–95). This illusion of facts hampered Fisher's work on index numbers, monetary theory, and proposals for monetary reform, as well as his understanding of the "new economic era" and Prohibition. A colleague of Fisher's at Yale, Ray Westerfield, developed this and other related points in a memorial article.

> Fisher was never content to stop with scientific research; he was imbued with an irresistible urge to reform, along lines indicated by his studies. For example, having seen and felt the evils of unstable money and having discovered the causes and cures, he was determined to do all he could to make it stable.
>
> Unfortunately his eagerness to promote his cause sometimes had a bad influence on his scientific attitude. It distorted his judgement; for example, he was carried away by his "new economic era" ideas in the late 1920s and lost his fortune. . . . He relied upon concomitancy too much in his belief that the stability of the price level from 1925 to 1929 was due to Federal Reserve action and refused to give due recognition to other factors at work. (Quoted in I. N. Fisher 1956, 193)

Fisher's conclusions and convictions guided the statistical studies that gave him faith in the attainment of his goals in matters of monetary policy and prohibition. The fall of Prohibition at the bottom of the Great Depression must have made for dark days for this well-intentioned reformer. He retired from academic life shortly thereafter but continued as an active reformer and contributor to public debate.

PROHIBITION'S BLUE MONDAY

While Fisher was beginning to realize some of the negative consequences of Prohibition, professional economists and the general public were becoming increasingly aware of the costs and ineffectiveness of the "noble experiment." Two noteworthy examples of economists who examined Prohibition and found Fisher's position less than accurate were Clark Warburton and Herman Feldman.

In *Prohibition: Its Economic and Industrial Aspects* (1930) Herman Feldman, an otherwise undistinguished economist, published an important contribution to the statistical investigation of the "economic" aspects of Prohibition.[11] His book is based on twenty articles written for the *Christian Science Monitor*, and the statistical information derives from a detailed survey. The book is most impressive in its caution concerning the use of survey data, statistical analysis, and the conclusions made throughout the book.

His book is noteworthy for its criticism of Fisher's estimate of the economic loss due to the consumption of alcohol, despite the fact that Feldman was writing for the *Christian Science Monitor*, a champion of Prohibition.

Even the writings on prohibition by some distinguished economists show a certain freedom from scientific restraint not normally found in their discussions of other subjects. One of the most curiously constructed statistical statements, for example, is that by which Professor Irving Fisher, of Yale, deduces that prohibition has been worth at least $6,000,000,000 a year to this country. This figure, widely quoted, has often been used as if it were a painstaking, scientific calculation based on a meticulous combing of economic data. On the contrary, it is merely a guess, and of a type frequently issued by groups with propaganda in mind, but hardly to be expected from one who has achieved world-wide prominence as a statistical economist. (Feldman 1930, 5)

Fisher's estimate was based on uncontrolled experiments on the effect of alcohol on industrial efficiency. These experiments were made on one to five individuals who took strong doses of alcohol on an empty stomach before beginning work. These "studies," some of which were based solely on the effects of alcohol on the experimenter himself, found that average efficiency was reduced by 2 percent per drink. Fisher then assumed a dosage of five drinks per day and extrapolated the loss of total efficiency per worker to a 10 percent reduction in efficiency. *If* alcohol consumption by workers could be reduced to zero, Fisher estimated, the country could save at least 5 percent of total income, or $3,300,000,000. The elimination of the alcohol industry would also save an additional 5 percent in national income as resources would be transferred out of alcohol

---

[11]A search of the *Index of Economic Journals* showed Herman Feldman's contributions were limited to two review articles and four monographs on labor policy.

production and into other goods and services. Feldman noted that a 2 percent loss in efficiency could be caused by "a mere depressing thought," and that Fisher failed to account for the fact that most alcohol consumed by the working class was beer with meals hours before work. Indeed, historical experience suggests that alcohol was consumed on the job in order to increase the overall efficiency of production. "It will require experiments on a far larger scale, and under much more rigorously controlled conditions than those now recorded, to determine the effect of alcoholic beverages upon industrial efficiency with the definiteness expressed. The experiments, considered solely as bases for the economic calculations made [by Fisher], are inconclusive of themselves" (Feldman 1930, 240–41).

Feldman was also known for his survey of absenteeism. He surveyed industrialists concerning the absence or tardiness of workers on Mondays and the days following paydays. The survey asked whether the respondents felt Prohibition was the cause of any noticeable reduction in absenteeism. Information on the relationship between alcohol consumption and absenteeism prior to Prohibition was not available.[12] Of the 287 responses to Feldman's survey, less than half felt that there was considerable improvement in absenteeism. One-third of the respondents who did detect decreased absenteeism failed to attribute this improvement to Prohibition. Some employers even reported higher absenteeism and attributed the increase to Prohibition. One employer noted that "the stuff available to labor, and there is plenty of it, is so rotten that it takes the drinking man two or three days to get over his spree" (Feldman 1930, 211).

Feldman himself described some of the faults of the survey method, such as personal or political bias in completing the forms, and he cautioned against a strict interpretation of the results. Other points of contention with the conclusions of the survey were that private prohibition and stricter employer liability and negligence laws all contributed greatly to reducing absenteeism. Improved safety conditions, higher wage rates, reduced working hours, and more formal labor contracts also improved attendance. On the other

---

[12]A Boston rubber company which employed almost 10,000 workers reported that company nurses made 30,000 visits in 1925 but could not state with any certainty that alcohol was the cause in more than six cases (Feldman 1930, 203).

Table 1. Absenteeism Rates in a Delaware Gunpowder Plant

Day	1907	1913	1924	1929
Monday	7.41	6.17	3.66	2.35
Tuesday	6.89	5.22	2.86	2.10
Wednesday	5.77	5.49	2.90	2.15
Thursday	5.68	5.06	2.37	2.01
Friday	5.38	5.05	2.10	1.89
Saturday	6.94	6.59	3.93	2.95
Average for week	6.35	5.59	2.96	2.24

Source: Warburton 1932, 205.

hand, booming standards of living and new leisure alternatives, such as the automobile, also influenced absenteeism during the 1920s.

Feldman obtained only one company's records on absenteeism that contained data from before and after Prohibition. He noted that the company which supplied this information indicated that the improvement in attendance was *not* due to Prohibition but rather to improvement in labor. His data along with the 1929 update provided by the Bureau of Prohibition are presented in table 1.

Feldman's cautions and clarifications concerning the data were not sufficient to prevent the data from being used to support the case for the economic benefits of Prohibition enforcement. "All of us know that industrial efficiency was one of the chief reasons for Prohibition" (I. Fisher 1927, 158). The report of the National Commission on Law Observance and Enforcement (1931) began the section on the economic benefits of Prohibition with the statement: "The subjects upon which there is objective and reasonably trustworthy *proof* are industrial benefits—i.e., increased production, increased efficiency of labor, elimination of 'blue Monday,' and decrease in industrial accidents" (71). The report goes on to emphasize the reliability of these facts with respect to absenteeism: "There is strong and convincing evidence, supporting the view of the greater number of large employers, that a notable increase in production, consequent upon increased efficiency of labor and elimination of the chronic absences of great numbers of workers after Sundays and holidays, is directly attributable to doing away with saloons" (71).

The Bureau of Prohibition took Feldman's data one step further by obtaining data for 1929 and publishing the results in *The Value of*

Law Observance (1930, 11). These data were purported to show the decline of "blue Monday" as evidence of the economic benefits of Prohibition.

Americans were becoming increasingly aware that while Prohibition had eliminated the open saloon, it had not stopped the liquor traffic. The costs of enforcing Prohibition were increasing, and economic prosperity, purportedly the main benefit of Prohibition, ended with the stock-market crash in 1929. Establishing the link between Prohibition and reduced absenteeism was vital to sustaining public support of the policy.

By far the most thorough study of Prohibition was by Clark Warburton. His two main contributions were *The Economic Results of Prohibition* (1932) and his entry on Prohibition in the *Encyclopedia of the Social Sciences* (1934).[13] Warburton's book was initiated at the request of the Association against the Prohibition Amendment, from which he received financial support during the early stages of his investigation.[14]

Warburton's book was a statistical analysis of the economic arguments for and against Prohibition. Primarily he examined alcohol consumption, expenditures on alcohol, and the impact of Prohibition on industrial efficiency, public health, income and demographic groups, and public finance. He used all available statistics, produced estimates from underlying conditions, and in many cases used more than one estimating technique. Warburton cautiously alerted his reader to weak links in estimation techniques and data collection.[15] "In these circumstances no study of the results of prohibition can claim high precision and unquestionable proof. The conclusions stated here can claim, however, to be reasonable inferences, after

---

[13]It is particularly interesting that Warburton was chosen to produce the entry on Prohibition, as Irving Fisher was one of the editors of the *Encyclopedia*.

[14]Despite the role of this special-interest group in initiating this study, several prominent economists read and commented on the final work. Warburton thanks Wesley C. Mitchell, Harold Hotelling, Joseph Dorfman, and Arthur Burns for comments and advice in the preface.

[15]Warburton does not appear to have been building a case against prohibition; for example, he omitted all discussion of the increasing cost of prisons and the congestion of the court system directly attributable to the enforcement of Prohibition.

intensive study and analysis, from such data as are available" (Warburton 1932, 259).

Warburton concluded that consumption of all alcohol per capita
declined nearly one-third from 1911–14 to 1927–30, but that consumption of spirits increased 10 percent during the same period. He
found that expenditures for alcohol during Prohibition were
approximately equal to what expenditures would have been had the
pre-Prohibition conditions existed.[16] Expenditures on beer fell dramatically, while expenditures on distilled spirits increased. He was
unable to establish correlations between Prohibition and prosperity,
saving, insurance costs, or the purchase of consumer durables.

Warburton found that the data did not show a measurable relationship between Prohibition and the decrease in industrial accidents. He also found that Prohibition had no measurable effect on
the observed increase in industrial productivity and that statistical
evidence was lacking to establish the influence of Prohibition on
industrial absenteeism. With regard to Feldman's survey, Warburton
noted that the reduction in absenteeism was more plausibly the result
of the reduction in the number of hours worked and the lightening
of actual work tasks (less manual, more mechanical), as well as the
introduction of new and greater quantities of recreational and leisure
activities as substitutes for alcohol.[17]

Warburton went on to criticize the applicability of the data on
absenteeism from the single gunpowder plant that was cited by the
government in support of the economic benefits of Prohibition.
Using the original data, Warburton calculated the average annual
percentage decline in absenteeism (table 2). He showed that the
annual percentage decline in absenteeism on Mondays did not differ

---

[16]He notes that the estimates for expenditures fall within a wide range, plus
or minus one-quarter to one-third based on the underlying assumptions of the
estimates. Proponents of Prohibition, such as Feldman 1930 and later T. Y. Hu
1950, argued that the estimates were too high, but modern experience with
the prohibition of marijuana would probably produce the exact opposite reaction (i.e., that they were too low).

[17]Warburton noted that the length of the average work week had declined
dramatically since Prohibition began. It should also be noted that real wage
rates increased significantly from the prewar years to the late 1920s. Higher
wages normally result in a more responsible workforce and a higher opportunity cost of leisure, especially when the work week is shorter.

Table 2. Average Annual Percentage-Point Decline in
Absenteeism in a Delaware Gunpowder Plant

Day	1907–13	1913–24	1924–29
Monday	0.21	0.23	0.26
Tuesday	0.28	0.21	0.15
Wednesday	0.05	0.24	0.15
Thursday	0.10	0.24	0.15
Friday	0.06	0.27	0.04
Saturday	0.06	0.24	0.20
Total	0.76	1.43	0.87

Source: Warburton 1932, 205.

much in the pre–Prohibition period, the transitional period, and the
Prohibition period. It seems the reduction of absenteeism is difficult
to attribute to Prohibition but easy to associate with other factors,
such as the reduction of the work week, increased real wages (during
the 1920s), and improved labor–management techniques.[18]

Greater experience with Prohibition resulted in increasing skepti-
cism among economists. This trend can be traced to three factors.
First, the black market continued to grow and develop despite
increased enforcement efforts and reorganization of the Prohibition
bureaucracy. Second, as data were collected over a longer period,
trends of increased consumption and crime became evident. Third,
the longer Prohibition was enforced, the more knowledge spread
concerning the adverse consequences and the difficulty of enforcement (also see Thornton 1991 B for more details concerning the
results of alcohol prohibition).

THE ECONOMICS OF HEROIN PROHIBITION

The sale of heroin and other opiates has been illegal at the federal
level since the passage of the Harrison Narcotics Act in 1914. Most
states had already enacted prohibitions and restrictions on these
products prior to the federal legislation. While narcotics were mentioned by economists such as Patten, Veblen, and Fisher, economists

---

[18]The average national work week declined 3.14 percent in the pre–Prohibition period, 9.19 percent in the transitional period, and did not change in the
Prohibition period (Warburton 1932, 205).

paid little attention to narcotic prohibition for the first fifty years of its existence. Simon Rottenberg's article (1968) on the economics of illegal heroin was published at a time when the general public and social scientists were beginning to examine the results of this prohibition.

In his seminal article Rottenberg (1968) described the options available to authorities, noting some of the factors that influence the activities of the law-enforcement bureaucracy. He also described the market structure, organization, and competitive forces but seemed to find the application of traditional economic analysis to the illegal market for heroin difficult because of the market's complex interaction with law enforcement. As a result, Rottenberg raised more questions than he answered.

Rottenberg found the heroin market more organized and monopolized than other illegal markets. He examined the impact of crime on society, particularly in connection with the allocation of police resources. Society faces a trade-off between enforcing narcotics laws and enforcing other criminal laws. Rottenberg detailed the corruption and the corruptive process in illegal drug markets and at one point anticipated James Buchanan's argument for organized crime.[19]

A theme that hindered Rottenberg's analysis was that the product which defined the market changed as it moved from production to consumption. He noted that heroin was diluted as it passed through the distribution chain to the consumer and that the final product was subject to wide variations in potency. He offered three hypotheses to explain changes in potency. The first, which he considered questionable, was that consumers were very responsive to price changes but not to changes in potency. His second hypothesis held that lowering potency was a rationing device when heroin was in short supply. While this may help explain the variation in potency, it does not explain either the systematic changes or "the apparent secular tendency for dilution to occur" that Rottenberg noted. The third hypothesis was that dilution allowed for differentiation of the product so that the consumer could be better served. Again, Rottenberg found this hypothesis unsatisfactory in explaining an important trend. On the subject of drug potency, Rottenberg noted: "It is like

---

[19]See Buchanan 1973, 119–32. Also see Sisk 1982 for a criticism of this view.

explaining why Falcon automobiles will be manufactured, as well as Continentals, but would not explain why the fraction of Falcons rises and the fraction of Continentals falls" (1968, 83).

In summary, Rottenberg's contribution is descriptive and institutional, but it contains little of lasting theoretical or empirical value. He developed more questions than answers, but this is precisely why his contribution is important. Answers to his questions, extensions of some of his points, and corrections of others characterize much of the research on prohibition since the publication of his article.

Two noteworthy comments that raised important matters of substance and questioned the basic validity of prohibition followed Rottenberg's article. Edward Erickson (1969) indicated that efforts to decrease the supply of euphoric drugs resulted in important social costs, such as higher production costs per unit of euphoria produced, increasing redistribution of income through theft by addicts, and debasement of drug-law enforcement. Given these costs, society should move to less enforcement.

Raul A. Fernandez (1969) discussed two related points concerning the market for heroin that Rottenberg did not explicitly examine. First, the status of heroin addicts as user-sellers leads to important difficulties and complexities in applying economic theory to this market. Addiction is also important for Fernandez because addiction reduces the deterrent effect of prison sentences. It is the question of addiction to heroin which would lead economists again to question the fundamental axiom of individual rationality in connection with the use of illegal "addicting" drugs. Fernandez suggests that the proper approach to addiction is not prohibition but treatment for addiction.[20]

Mark H. Moore (1977) provides a detailed analysis of the illicit market for heroin and law enforcement in New York City.[21] His

---

[20]Fernandez attempts to estimate the benefits of rehabilitating heroin addicts, and he explores the Marxian approach to heroin addiction (1971, 1973). He applies class analysis to the understanding of the origins of narcotics legislation and the allocation of enforcement resources to crime/class categories. He also inquires into the role of neoclassical (purely formal) rationality, modern approaches to criminology, and the Marxian notion of lumpenproletariat (the poor), for the study of addiction and prohibition. Also see Bookstaber 1976 on the market for addictive drugs.

[21]Also see Moore 1973, 1976.

analysis uses economic theory, law and law-enforcement analysis, and direct empirical observation of the workings of the heroin market in New York City. These tools allow Moore to present a realistic picture of the complexities of the heroin market and to debunk several commonly held beliefs concerning the illicit heroin market. Indeed, his work represents what is now the conventional wisdom on public policy toward the heroin market.

Prior to Moore's study, conventional wisdom said that the demand for heroin was perfectly inelastic and that higher prices would not result in decreased consumption. Higher prices served only to increase the costs to society and the profits for drug dealers. Higher profits stimulated drug dealership and new consumption, and therefore worked against the goals of public policy.[22] Moore effectively argues against both the assumption of perfectly inelastic demand and the notion that drug dealers are better off as a result of increased law enforcement (1977, 5–15).

Moore recommends effective regulation of heroin by continuing the current policy of prohibition.[23] In raising the effective price of heroin, prohibition discourages "not-yet users" from trying the drug, but has only a marginal effect on "current users." Moore notes that heroin use is initiated and spread through friends and neighborhood groups and that it is difficult for law enforcement to infiltrate these tight-knit groups. He postulates that if access to heroin could be prevented by raising the cost of acquiring heroin, the spread of heroin use could be stopped and "not-yet users" discouraged from trying the drug.

It is erroneous, however, to claim that prohibition is necessary to discourage access to heroin because of the particular system by which it spreads (small social groups) when prohibition itself is responsible for this system. Moore himself argues that it is prohibition that is responsible for the peculiar organization of the illegal heroin market: "It is almost certain that the single most important

---

[22]Moore cites Phares 1973 and Votey and Phillips 1976 as representative of the conventional analysis.

[23]Moore notes, "Effectively prohibiting heroin (i.e., eliminating all supplies of heroin) is impossible without unacceptable expenditures and intolerable assaults on civil liberties. Hence, regulation is a more appropriate and feasible objective than prohibition" (1977, xxi).

factor influencing the structure of heroin-distribution systems is that producing, importing, selling, and possessing heroin are all prohibited in the United States. Why, for example, isn't the industry organized into larger and *more impersonal marketing systems?*" (1977, 3; emphasis added). Further, he makes no attempt to justify prohibition as the only or best way of preventing consumers from experimenting with heroin.[24]

Moore recommends that a variety of programs be established for current users of heroin. He recognizes that prohibition is harmful to current users and that higher prices lead addicts to inflict costs on the general population in the form of muggings, robbery, and burglary. To avoid these problems, Moore recommends that addicts be given a low-cost source of heroin or methadone; that addicts have access to treatment facilities, jobs, reasonable living standards, recreation, and entertainment; and that arrested users be allowed to enter treatment facilities rather than prison (1977, 258–61).

Moore's reasons for trying to reduce the effects of prohibition on current users are well founded. His recommendations are flawed in several respects, however. His attempt to establish price discrimination would have important drawbacks and be difficult to carry out. For example, his recommendations would reduce the cost of becoming an addict and therefore would act to stimulate experimentation with heroin. Moore himself recognizes the contradiction in his policy recommendations:

Note that the dilemma faced in enforcing narcotics laws is common to all negative incentive systems. The problem is fundamental: The desire to have the incentive conflicts with the desire to minimize the damage done to people who do not respond to the incentive. One cannot lessen the adverse effects on current users without having some effect on the magnitude of the incentives facing nonusers. One cannot alter the incentives facing nonusers without having some effect on the consequences for current users. (1977, 237)

Moore's recommendations would also involve large increases in government expenditures. His claims that there is general support

---

[24]Articles by various authors reprinted in Morgan 1974 suggest that prior to opiate prohibition, addiction and use spread from doctors and druggists. Morgan himself suggests that little has changed since the prohibition of narcotics in terms of the size of the American addict population.

for the policy of prohibition (1977, xxi) fail to give adequate consideration to the taxpayers' toleration of the cost of his recommendations.

With respect to prohibition, Moore seems to be his own best critic:

> The single, most important objective of a narcotics-enforcement strategy is to discourage people who are not now using heroin from beginning to do so. If the police cannot achieve this objective at a reasonable cost in terms of public resources and maintenance of civil liberties, the prohibition policy ought to be abandoned. There are too many bad side effects of the policy and too few direct benefits other than preventing new use to warrant continuation of the policy if it cannot discourage new use. (1977, 238)

Finally, Moore reminds his reader that his study focused on but one illegal drug within New York City and, further, that his methodology was insufficient completely to analyze the problem at hand:

> There are serious limitations to the methodology employed in this book. The methodology is similar to that used in developing intelligence estimates. Bits of unverified, half-verified, and fully verified information are assembled into a systematic picture by combining arbitrary definitions with assumptions about how reasonable men behave. . . . It [the methodology employed] has the disadvantage of providing only good guesses about the nature of the phenomenon. Moreover, the guesses may be radically altered by the introduction of a single, verified piece of information. (1977, 4)

Therefore, while Moore's contribution is important in extending the literature concerning the heroin market, weaknesses in methodology and scope undermine the applicability of his policy recommendations.[25] By defeating the conventional approach of the 1960s, Moore reestablished the viability of prohibition as a policy to control heroin use.

---

[25]Clague 1973 provides an ordinal ranking of five public policies toward heroin based on seven criteria: crime, number of addicts, well-being of addicts, police corruption, police violation of civil liberties, legal deprivation of traditional liberties, and respect for the law. The policies evaluated include prohibition, methadone maintenance (strict and permissive), heroin maintenance, and quarantine. By and large, heroin maintenance received the highest marks and prohibition received the lowest marks.

THE ECONOMICS OF ADDICTION

The history of economic thought is strewn with attacks on individual rationality.[26] The consumer has been criticized for consuming on the basis of imperfect information, as well as not consuming because of imperfect information (that is, hoarding). The consumer has been criticized for steadfastly maintaining a consumption plan despite changing circumstances, problems, and severe difficulties (habits, addictions), as well as not maintaining established consumption plans due to changing circumstances, information, and evaluations (impulse buying, binging). According to Israel Kirzner, "The concept of rationality in human behavior has long been a topic for discussion in the literature on the methodology of economics. Attacks on the undue reliance which economic theory has been accused of placing upon human reason are as old as attacks on the very notion of an economic theory" (Kirzner 1976, 167).

The irrationality claim has been made with respect to addictive goods such as alcohol and narcotics since at least the time of Vilfredo Pareto. Pareto made a distinction (similar to Fisher's) between logical actions, which are rational and economic, and illogical actions, which are not. Irrational action was found in the case of a man who established a detailed budget devoid of wine expenditures and then proceeded to binge on wine. Benedetto Croce explained that this act was an economic error because the man yielded to a temporary desire at odds with his established plans.[27] Such notions of logic and rationality are primary theoretical justifications for prohibition. The type of "irrationality" described by Raul Fernandez (1969), however, forms a basis of attack, rather than a justification for prohibition.

In defining the Chicago school's position on tastes, George S. Stigler and Gary S. Becker (1977) have also commented on the nature of addiction. They find that beneficial and harmful addictions depend on whether prolonged use enhances or diminishes future

---

[26]While rationality is fundamental to most schools of thought, it should be recognized that the meaning of rationality and the role it plays in economic analysis differs from school to school. See, for example, Becker 1962, 1963. Also see Kirzner 1962, 1963.

[27]See Croce 1953, 177. For an early critique of Croce see Tagliacozzo 1945. For a general discussion and modern critique see Kirzner 1976, 167–72; 1979, 120–33.

consumption. Good addictions involve the consumption of goods, such as classical music, that increase utility over time and do not disrupt utility derived from other goods. Bad addictions involve a reduction in future consumption ability. Alcohol decreases future utility because it reduces the utility of a given amount of future consumption as well as the utility from other goods. Addiction is a rational habit that is consistent with preferences and opportunities but one that hinges on the type of capital effect the good produces.[28]

Thomas A. Barthold and Harold M. Hochman (1988) contest Stigler and Becker's view of the rational addict: "Whether addiction is rational behavior . . . seems beside the point" (90). They begin with the premise that addictive behavior is extreme behavior, "neither normal or typical."[29] They find that compulsion is the driving force behind addiction, but that an individual must be an "extreme seeker" for compulsion to develop into addiction. Consumption can have capital effects that will cause irreversible harm if they pass a certain threshold.

Barthold and Hochman attempt to model multiperiod, multiplan, multiprice consumption by identifying addiction with concave indifference curves (atypical preferences). They find that changes in relative prices can lead to corner solutions (peculiar consumption decisions), that consumption decisions are "sticky" at low prices, and that consumption can lead to addiction.

Robert J. Michaels (1988) models compulsive behavior through an integration of the psychological literature on addiction with the consumption model developed by Kelvin Lancaster (1966). Self-esteem is entered into the addict's utility function. Michaels is then able to explain many of the observed behavioral patterns associated with addiction, such as the ineffectiveness of treatment programs, the agony of withdrawal, radical changes by the addict (such as conversion to religion), the use of substitutes, and the typical addiction pattern of use, discontinuation, and backsliding.

---

[28]For a full development of integration of habits into neoclassical economic analysis, see Ault and Ekelund 1988.

[29]They find it neither typical nor normal despite the fact that they cite figures to suggest that heroin use among American soldiers during the Vietnam War was typical. They also cite figures which suggest that while no particular addiction is common throughout the population, some form of addiction or compulsion is normal, whether it be to wine, mystery novels, or chocolate.

The interpretation of consumer behavior in the Lancastrian consumption technology reasserts the rationality of choice by addicts. In addition, it does so without assuming unusual preferences of consumers or unusual properties of the "addictive" good.[30] Michaels finds that prohibition is an inconsistent policy with respect to addictive behavior in the sense that a policy that attempts "to convince users that they are losers is more likely to fail . . . and may induce increases in the level at which it [consumption] is undertaken" (1988, 85). The model is lacking in several respects, however. It does not consider the supply side of the market (either legal or illegal), nor does it consider problems such as the externalities of the addict's behavior.[31] Finally, Michaels bases the utility function on one current understanding of addictive behavior, which, he points out, is subject to change.[32]

Gary S. Becker and Kevin M. Murphy (1988) further develop the theory of rational addiction as introduced by Stigler and Becker (1977), in which rationality means a consistent plan to maximize utility over time. Their model relies on "unstable steady states" to understand addiction rather than on plan-alteration through time. They use consumption capital effects, adjacent complementarity between present and future consumption, time preference, and the effect of permanent versus temporary price changes to explain such nonnormal behavior as addiction, binges, and the decision to quit cold turkey.

Becker and Murphy note, "Addiction is a major challenge to the theory of rational behavior" (1988, 695). They claim it challenges

---

[30]Michaels criticizes Barthold and Hochman's (1988) assumptions about consumer preferences "that there are a small number of repellent people in the world whose preferences are characterized by an extreme nonconvexity. Such an assumption would seldom be found acceptable in other areas of economics. Fortunately it is not needed here" (Michaels 1988, 86–87).

[31]Michaels addresses many of these points (1987, 289–326).

[32]As Barthold and Hochman (1988, 91) point out: "Psychologists and sociologists claim little success in describing an 'addictive personality,' finding at most that 'alcoholics (and drug addicts) appear . . . different from others,' according to Lang (1983, 207); but not in a discernible, systematic way (at least from the variable they examine)." There is currently a debate between the disease approach and the free-will approach to addiction. Within the free-will camp there is a disagreement on whether addiction represents a loss of will or simply the lack of it.

both the Chicago approach to rational behavior and the general approach to rationality in which individuals attempt to maximize utility *at all times*. Becker and Murphy successfully defend Chicago rationality and are able, through changes in economic variables, to explain behavior associated with addiction. The introduction of unstable steady states defends rational behavior against Croce's original criticism and represents a marginal move toward the Austrian notion of rationality. In the Austrian view, plans are made by individuals under conditions of limited information and uncertainty. Plans are made at points in time, but *choice cannot be independent of actual choice*. Becker and Murphy adjust their notion of rationality from one of "a consistent plan to maximize utility over time" (1988, 675) to one where " 'rational' means that individuals maximize utility consistently over time" (1988, 694).

This literature explores the question of rationality with respect to addiction and dangerous drugs. For the most part, it shares the common heritage of the Chicago tradition. Rationality is a crucial issue for both prohibition and economic theory in general. While this literature is in general agreement with Fernandez on the difficulty of making prohibition work, its conclusions are based on the rationality of the consumer rather than the lack of it. As a result, prohibition is found to be costly, inconsistent, incomplete, or of limited value.

2

The Origins of Prohibition

The strange phenomenon of Prohibition, after an appearance
amongst us of over three years, is still non-understandable to
the majority of a great, and so-called free, people. It is one of
the most astonishing manifestations the world has ever witnessed. It came upon us like a phantom, swiftly; like a thief in
the night, taking us by surprise. Yet the Prohibitionists will tell
you that no one should be amazed, since for years—for almost
a century—quiet forces have been at work to bring about this
very thing.
—Charles Hanson Towne, *The Rise and Fall of Prohibition*

The episode of national alcohol prohibition is one of the most
intriguing in American history. As Charles Hanson Towne
(1923) suggests, the prohibition movement began long before the
constitutional measure was ever contemplated. Alcohol was the stim-
ulus of the entire prohibitionist movement, which promoted the use
of the state to stamp out sin and impurity in order to shore up free will
against the ravages of individualism. Present prohibitions against
narcotics and the movement to outlaw alcohol and tobacco originated
in the nineteenth-century battle against alcohol.

Two aspects of the origins of prohibition play major roles in the
current politics of prohibition. First, prohibitionists believe that, once
started, prohibitions are difficult to stop. Even some opponents of
prohibition view legalization as undesirable because, they believe,
addiction and crime in illegal markets will spread throughout society.
Second, opponents of prohibition allege that it is an attempt by a

majority to discriminate against certain minorities. Evidence of such discrimination undercuts the moral authority of prohibition and brings into question the public-spirited aims of prohibitionists.

In addition to these issues, answers to a number of important questions are necessary for a fuller understanding of the political economy of prohibition. For example, What is the source of the demand for prohibition? How are prohibitions adopted as public policy? What factors explain why some prohibitions become stable (narcotics) while others do not (alcohol)?

I will use an interest-group approach to answer these questions. The advances made by Bruce Benson (1984) and Jennifer Roback (1989) enable an explanation of prohibition which captures both the profit-seeking motives of firms and industry associations, as well as the "non-pecuniary gains" and "psychic rents" pursued by reform groups. The success of prohibition rests on the ability of "public-spirited" groups, commercial interests, professional organizations, and bureaucracies to form effective coalitions against consumers and producers of certain products.

Crucial for determining and evaluating the direction of public policy is the source of the "public-spirited" purpose of prohibition. Before Prohibition, the markets for alcohol, narcotics, marijuana, and tobacco were not free. Tobacco products were prohibited in many states during the 1920s. (See J. E. Brooks [1952] concerning intervention on tobacco.) On the contrary, they were the most heavily regulated and taxed markets in the economy. Much of the well-intentioned discontent with the consumption of these products will be shown to be linked to these regulatory policies.

THE PROHIBITION OF ALCOHOL

The development of prohibitionism will be broken down into three periods. The birth of prohibition covers the period from colonial times to the Civil War. The politicalization and growth of prohibitionism occurs from the Civil War to about 1900. The adoption of national prohibitions occurs during the Progressive Era, roughly 1900–1920. The national prohibition of marijuana, which did not occur until 1937, is treated as a consequence of the adoption of alcohol and narcotics prohibition and the repeal of alcohol prohibition.

The Early American Experience

In colonial America alcohol was generally viewed as a normal and practical matter. Three exceptions to this rule provide lessons concerning the control of alcohol consumption.

First, while alcohol was an accepted part of society, the Puritan ethic did discourage excessive use of alcohol. Puritans established sumptuary legislation designed to limit alcohol consumption and to prohibit tobacco consumption. This type of legislation was found to be ineffective and self-defeating and was later abolished (Weeden [1890] 1963 and North 1988).

Second, legislation was passed to prevent the sale of alcohol to Indians, slaves, servants, and apprentices. These restrictions proved to be ineffective and in some cases counterproductive. Free laborers were often provided alcohol rations on the job, while slaves, servants, and apprentices were told to do without. This encouraged them to run away from their masters or to consume alcohol under seedy conditions. The prohibition against selling alcohol to Indians was often avoided, overlooked, or repealed, because liquor opened up valuable opportunities in the fur trade.[1]

Third, the colony of Georgia was organized as an experimental society by George Oglethorpe to promote temperance. In 1735, restrictions were placed on spirits, and subsidies were provided for beer. This experiment proved successful only with German immigrants, who were grateful for the subsidy on beer. The colony's wood and raw materials were most eagerly demanded in the West Indies, which could offer little other than rum in exchange (Boorstin 1958, 91–92). The smuggling of rum proved to be an easy task, and even those apprehended had little to fear because juries regularly acquitted violators of the law (Krout 1925, 56–59).

Other methods of intervention into the sale of alcohol were licensing and protectionism, prominent features of the mercantilist philosophy. The license system provided local monopolies on the sale of alcohol in most of colonial America. Such monopolies were granted to innkeepers in order to encourage innkeeping, control the distribution of alcohol, and provide government revenue.

---

[1]This prohibition benefited fur traders willing to circumvent it, which might explain its existence.

Inns were associated with the extension of trade, economic development, and higher standards of living. They were a place where circuit judges held court, where public meetings were held, and where public discussion and voting took place. Therefore, by encouraging innkeeping, the license system was viewed as an aid to economic, judicial, and political development. This system, however, often benefited political insiders who had an advantage in obtaining these licenses through "good public standing" provisions.

Corruption, poor service, and inferior products were often the result of this system of monopoly. Regulations were established regarding the quality and quantity of accommodations of these inns. As innkeepers reduced unprofitable (but required) services and the quality of their products (lodging, food, alcohol), elaborate regulations detailing the quality and prices of alcohol were established. Despite stringent penalties, these regulations proved difficult to monitor and enforce. It is ironic that the type of institution that this legislation promoted—the saloon—would become the central focus of the Prohibition cause.

Protectionist legislation was enacted in several states and localities to promote distilling and brewing. Alcohol was a remarkably important product in domestic and international trade. According to Harold Underwood Faulkner (1924, 94), "our forefathers were hard drinkers." Alcohol rations were given to soldiers and laborers as a practical matter of the labor contract and economic custom. Distilling rum was an important business in America. According to John Spenser Bassett (1932, 141), 1,260,000 gallons of rum were produced annually in the Boston area during the early eighteenth century. Rum was a vital component of the triangular trade between the slave coast of Africa, the West Indies sugar plantations, and the rum-producing areas in America.

John Allen Krout concludes:

On the eve of the Revolution, then, spirituous liquor was one of the greatest factors in moving colonial commerce. In whatever branch of trade the merchant invested his capital he relied upon rum or some other form of ardent spirits to earn profits for him. Since the traffic in intoxicants was consistently profitable for all who engaged in it, the public accorded it that approbation which attaches to most things indispensable to the world of business. Nothing short of a revolution in public opinion could remove it from its important place in American life. (1925, 50)

As Krout notes, it was high-potency alcohol that dominated the early American experience with alcohol, although the "ardent spirits" that dominated the market were of poor quality by modern standards. Storage and transportation considerations gave rum, and later whiskey, a natural advantage over beer, and brewers and malt were scarce and therefore expensive. Whiskey was easier to transport than both beer and grain, and whiskey could be stored much longer than beer.

In addition to these natural conditions, a plethora of government interventions distorted this market. Protectionist measures, subsidies, and local monopolies tended to promote the production of alcohol products, while taxation and regulations tended to control their use. Regulation and licensing were repressive forces on the development of alcohol. Monopoly, taxation, and extensive intervention had predictable distortive effects on prices, quantities, product quality, consumer choice, and the quality of competition.[2]

From Temperance to Prohibition: Remember the Maine Laws

The economic advantage of strong drink combined with the abuses and distortions created by the license system generated increasing concern about intemperance in American society. Reformers began to see the license system as government support for alcohol rather than a control on consumption. Early reformers such as Cotton and Increase Mather, Benjamin Rush (a signer of the Declaration of Independence), and Lyman Beecher led the battle against intemperance. The Massachusetts Society for the Suppression of Intemperance was organized to contain the heavy drinking associated with the War of 1812, and the American Temperance Society was organized in 1826. The temperance movement would evolve into an effective movement that would establish prohibition in thirteen states and territories only to retreat during the development of the Republican party, the abolitionist movement, and the Civil War.

The temperance movement had grown to over a million members by 1833, consisting largely of northern evangelicals from the

---

[2]Military service, particularly in the Revolutionary War, increased individuals' desire to drink and exposed soldiers to strong drink and raucous behavior.

Baptist, Congregationalist, Methodist, and Presbyterian churches. Born in the revival movements of the 1820s and 1830s, evangelical Protestantism is best described as postmillennial pietism because its adherents believed that there would be a thousand-year kingdom of God on earth and that it was their job to prepare the world for Jesus' return. It is not surprising that as this group matured it turned increasingly to the power of the state to bolster the battle against alcohol. Ian R. Tyrrell (1979, 7) notes that in addition to the evangelical ministers and their flocks, young, upwardly mobile entrepreneurs supported temperance in order to improve the economy.

The Washingtonians were another important group within the temperance movement, consisting largely of former drinkers. They formed a voluntary organization to provide charity to drunkards and support for those who wished to abstain from drunkenness. The group was similar to Alcoholics Anonymous in organizational structure, membership, and principles. These activists attacked the use of legal suasion as a tactic and criticized the clergy for preaching to the converted upper classes, rather than working with those who needed their help the most. The Washingtonians donated more money to the needy than other temperance organizations, despite being generally of modest means. They attracted many members, raised lots of money, and converted many drunkards. The Washingtonian societies were later co-opted by the newly formed Sons of Temperance (a fraternal organization) and other temperance and prohibitionist organizations.[3]

It is useful to illustrate the transition from temperance to prohibition as a four-phase process. In the first phase, intemperance was understood as excessive drinking and drunkenness. The solution was to educate the public about the dangers of alcohol. Reformers stressed that spirits should be used in moderation and that education by example could achieve temperance in society. Beer and wine were generally of no or little concern to reformers at this time.

The second phase involved a turn toward abstinence from spirits. Again, this goal was to be achieved through voluntary means and education by example. It was during this phase that the temperance societies were formed and strengthened. The pledge of abstinence

---

[3]See Hampel 1982, chaps. 6–9.

became a prominent and important tool for the organization and radicalization of the temperance movement.

The next phase began as a battle between temperance forces. The new force that ultimately dominated was the radical element, which called for total abstinence from all alcoholic beverages, including beer and wine. This faction was initially viewed as a threat to social custom, individual liberty, and religious tradition, and as unnecessary to the achievement of temperance. The total-abstinence groups dominated other groups through superior organization, fund-raising, and recruitment of new members.

A concurrent development and debate ensued about the choice between voluntary and coercive means to achieve temperance. The traditional philosophy had been that the means to achieve temperance should be voluntary. Education, leading by example, and obtaining signatures on abstinence pledges were the tools of the temperance movement. The strategy was successful as measured by the number of members, the number of local groups, and the number of signers of the various abstinence pledges.

The coercive strategy, however, gained increasing attention and importance as temperance forces grew frustrated and impatient with the long and difficult process involved with their strategy. The conversion of nondrinkers, teetotalers, reformed alcoholics, and evangelical Protestants was relatively easy compared with the conversion of heavy drinkers and members of immigrant groups in which alcohol was part of social and religious custom. These impatient prohibitionists often blamed their frustration on the lure of alcohol and the profits that accrued to sellers of alcohol.

This phase represented a change in strategy toward the coercive means of government. The license system, which condoned alcohol use, was to be replaced by some form of direct restriction on alcohol consumption. The history of this phase is characterized by temperance forces organizing coalitions in order to pass restrictive legislation, such as local option, quantity sale requirements, and local prohibitions. These restrictions ultimately failed to achieve their intended results, proved difficult to enforce, and led to unintended consequences, such as increased intemperance, poor-quality alcohol, and the existence of unsavory drinking establishments.

The radical strategists were increasingly successful in establishing these interventionist measures. True temperance organizations such as the Washingtonians weakened while prohibitionists strengthened themselves politically through alliances with the abolitionist and anti-immigrant movements.

Interventionism, like the temperance organizations, was unable to establish total abstinence in society. After each failure, temperance groups would advocate more stringent policies. Typically, the radical strategy began with minimum-purchase requirements, then moved to local licensing options, and finally to local prohibitions.[4] Each of these measures either failed to achieve the desired result or proved difficult to enforce. Competitive pressures and the lure of profits kept the supply of alcohol flowing. It was this process that led to statewide prohibition in Maine in 1851 (Byrne 1969).

The author of the law, Neal Dow, promoted it as a model to be spread across the nation, and indeed many of the northern states and territories adopted the law between 1851 and 1855. In many cases "Maine laws" were simply stronger versions of existing laws against liquor. Maine laws allowed for search and seizure, reduced the requirements for conviction, increased fines, and called for mandatory imprisonment and destruction of captured liquor.

But the rapid success of this prohibition movement was short-lived. By 1880 only Vermont, Maine, and New Hampshire remained dry at the state level. Among the many reasons for the failure of the Maine laws was the opposition of Irish and German immigrants. These rapidly growing immigrant groups, as well as the drinking native population, opposed and often openly violated the prohibition.

The Maine laws suffered several setbacks in court. In many states the courts ruled that the laws or certain aspects of the law (especially the search and seizure aspects) were illegal. Ironically, the birth of the Republican party (political home for most prohibitionists) and the tide against slavery also reduced prohibitionism. Republicans understood that an outright embrace of prohibitionism would be divisive for the new party (William Gienapp 1987). The slavery issue was drawing an increasing amount of public attention away from the alcohol problem.

---

[4]Minimum-purchase restrictions required that a person buy at least a certain (large) quantity of spirits, such as fifteen gallons. The requirements were designed to discourage spirit consumption among the low- and middle-income classes.

By far the most telling aspect of the Maine laws was ineffective enforcement. Professional police forces existed in only a few large cities, which tended to be dominated by hard-drinking immigrant populations. This meant that prohibitionists would have to organize and finance enforcement efforts. The prohibitionists were initially active in enforcing the laws, but they found this costly. They also found that many drinkers simply did not accept the authority of democratically determined morality.

One notable event involved the father of the Maine law and mayor of Portland, Neal Dow. Dow was accused by opponents of personally profiting from the government-controlled sale of alcohol for industrial and medicinal purposes. As described by Tyrrell the confrontation between Dow and his accusers had a dramatic effect on the momentum of the prohibitionist movements:

An angry mob assembled at the liquor agency on the night of June 2, 1855, after the existence of the liquor had become common knowledge. The mob demanded destruction of the liquor and threatened to break into the agency if the demand were not met and Neal Dow arrested for violation of his own law. Dow, who was always quick to look to force in defense of morality, assembled the local Rifle Guards. In the confrontation which followed with the stone-throwing mob, Dow ordered his troops to fire when several rioters broke into the liquor agency. (1979, 295–99)

Dow was labeled a fanatic and a murderer (Byrne 1969, 60–69). The emerging distilling, brewing, and saloon interests made the "tyranny" of Dow and the Maine laws a major issue of subsequent elections, and the prohibition movement quickly retreated from political prominence.

The Coalition of Prohibition

The second half of the nineteenth century was a period of retrenchment and coalition building for the prohibitionist movement. After the defeat of the Confederacy and the "reconstruction" of the South, social reformers once again turned their full attention to eliminating evil spirits from society. (See Richard Jensen [1971; 1983] and Joel H. Silbey [1967; 1973; 1978] for the important political changes in the second half of the nineteenth century.)

The important parts of this reform movement consisted of the women's movement, the Prohibition party, the Anti-Saloon League,

and professional organizations. Structural changes within the major
political parties also provided a catalyst for national prohibition. As
was the case before the Civil War, evangelical Protestantism was a
central force in all these parts, and alcohol was but the leading villain
for a prohibitionist movement that was preparing the earth for the
coming of Jesus.

Women were an important source of support for prohibition.
The woman-suffrage movement, which was born before the Civil
War, reemerged in full bloom in 1869. In that year the National
Woman Suffrage Association and the American Woman Suffrage
Association were formed, and women received the right to vote in
the Wyoming and Utah territories. Several leaders of the suffrage
movement, such as Susan B. Anthony, Elizabeth Cady Stanton, and
Lucy Stone, were involved in the temperance movement (Rosenstone, Behr, and Lazarus 1984, 75). Between the suffragettes and the
female abolitionists, women swelled the ranks of prohibitionist
organizations.

In 1873 the Women's Christian Temperance Union was formed
to unite Protestant women behind the cause of prohibition. Women
believed that they would be the prime beneficiary of temperance
because intemperance was generally a male problem, more specifically, a husband problem (Grimes 1967, 78). Women also played a
prominent part in both the Prohibition party and the Anti-Saloon
League. The relationship between suffrage and prohibition was a
two-way street: prohibitionists and nativists supported woman suffrage because it was felt that women would vote for prohibition and
immigration restrictions (Grimes 1967, 140–44).

The formation of the Prohibition party in 1869 and its first presidential campaign were the most tangible manifestations of the politicalization of the temperance movement. The third oldest party in the
history of the United States is often characterized as ineffective and
of little importance to the Prohibition movement. This interpretation, however, overlooks the role of third-party movements: the
introduction of public policy, attraction of public attention to social
problems, accurate demonstration of voter preferences, creation of
pressure for changes in the major political parties, and provision of
political experience and training for reformers.

The Prohibition party was the first party to endorse prohibition
of alcohol, child-labor laws, direct election of senators, an income

tax, and woman suffrage. All these "reforms" were eventually incorporated into the platforms of the major parties and passed into law. Temperance advocates gained insight into politics and political experience, which they applied to later efforts. As late as 1926 the Prohibition party was a member of a coalition consisting of the Women's Christian Temperance Union, the Anti-Saloon League, and local organizations which defeated the Republican senator James Wadsworth of New York, a leading supporter of the repeal of Prohibition. Valdimer O. Key (1958, 171) discusses the division of labor between political parties and special-interest groups:

In the workings of the political system a division of labor occurs between political parties and pressure groups. This is not necessarily a clean-cut separation of functions. Parties perform some functions almost never undertaken by pressure groups; and some of the activities of groups—and perhaps most of the activities of many groups—concern matters that parties seldom take a position on. On the other hand, on some matters parties and at least some groups work either in collaboration or in opposition.

Given a division of labor between pressure groups and political parties, it would be easy to overlook the fundamental importance of this third party. Peter H. Odegard, however, one of the important historians of the Anti-Saloon League, points out: "It would, of course, be erroneous to minimize the importance of the Prohibition Party in creating dry sentiment. The long and persistent battle which it waged certainly made the League's fight less difficult" ([1928] 1966, 101–3). It would be appropriate to consider the Prohibition party an important component of the politicization and political success of the prohibition movement.

The presidential vote total of the Prohibition party rose from 0.05 percent in 1872 to 2.25 percent in 1892, peaking just before the state prohibition movement. States in which the Prohibition party had the most success were the ones in which prohibition was first enacted.[5] More important, the Prohibition party was draining votes away from the Republicans (Kleppner 1979, 246–48). Combined with Populist party victories and economic depression, the agitation of the Prohibition party helped bring about dramatic realignment of the major parties.

---

[5]See Blocker 1976, 44–47.

During the 1890s the Republicans dropped prohibition in favor of moderation and woman suffrage in order to compete for the growing German vote. At the same time, William Jennings Bryan won the presidential nomination of the Democratic party. Best known for his role in the Scopes trial and free-silver position, Bryan captured the Prohibition party and appealed to the pietistic Protestants of the West, Midwest, and South (Kleppner 1987, 108–13 and 1982).

The Anti-Saloon League and the Adoption of Prohibition

The growing recognition of the failure of party politics to establish national prohibition and the natural impatience of the reformers led to the formation of the Anti-Saloon League in 1895. The league was the political arm of the Baptist, Congregationalist, Methodist, and Presbyterian churches. It was the league that collected and directed the efforts of prohibitionists in order to take advantage of the opportunity World War I provided.

The church-dominated league consisted of a complex bureaucratic network supported by membership fees and individual donations. Its principal means of agitating for prohibition and local option was the operation of a publishing company that produced pamphlets and paid speakers to denounce alcohol from the pulpit at any available opportunity. The league itself described the campaign for prohibition as "the Church in action against the saloon" (Odegard 1960, 116).

The league grew quickly. Only two state organizations of the league had been established by 1895, but forty-two states or territories had local organizations by 1904 (Blocker 1976, 157). Odegard ([1928] 1966, 20–21) estimates that when Prohibition was enacted, the league had the cooperation of 30,000 churches and 60,000 agencies.

The activity of the league began with an emphasis on local option. This proved to be a successful strategy in establishing prohibition in rural areas and jurisdictions dominated by Protestants. The league later turned to statewide prohibition and intimidation of major-party candidates. It used the evangelical-prohibitionist vote to swing elections away from uncooperative candidates and toward supporters of their cause.

Despite its Yankee Republican origins, the prohibition movement and the league's success moved west and south. The South was becoming increasingly "Yankeefied" and evangelical. Odegard

([1928] 1966, 81) examined voting patterns and found that the league's support came overwhelmingly from Democrats in the South and Republicans in the North. The drive toward state prohibition succeeded largely in rural and Protestant states, such as those in the South that were over 80 percent rural and 80 percent Protestant and in the less populous states of the West. The states and large cities of the Northeast outside New England remained dominated by Irish Democrats and wet Republicans. Jack S. Blocker (1976, 238) indicates that Prohibition never represented the majority opinion, suggesting that the success of Prohibition was based on logrolling.

Actually the league relied on a variety of politically expedient strategies, including intimidation of political candidates and officeholders. By 1915 the league had completely split with the voluntary and educational efforts of temperance. It had become an organized effort by evangelical Protestant churches to use politics to coerce temperance through prohibition.

The league was often criticized for its tactics by supporters, the Prohibition party, and church groups, as well as its opponents. The league's strategy of political opportunism, consisting of large payments to professional reformers and the direct use of the pulpit for political purposes, was often criticized by member churches. The league's criticism of blacks and Catholics, comparing them to the Ku Klux Klan or characterizing them as noncitizens or nonhumans who would sell their vote for a drink, was also criticized.

According to Odegard (1966, 74), at the height of its propaganda campaign, the league was publishing forty tons of literature each month. This indirect approach was immune to the charges and restrictions levied on the direct approach of the alcohol industry. The alcohol industry was subject to the Corrupt Practices Act which was established to monitor lobbying efforts and to prevent corruption. However, the league did not file under the Corrupt Practices Act until after Prohibition had been enacted, and then only under protest. Odegard notes that "in failing to make returns [reports of contributions and activities] for the years 1910 to 1918 the national organization certainly violated the spirit of the Corrupt Practices Act and possibly the letter" (1966, 210). The league was therefore able to spend large sums of money (as much as $2,500,000 per year) to promote its cause without coming under the same public scrutiny as the alcohol industry (Odegard 1966, 181).

The league's fund-raising success was based in part on its organization of business support against alcohol. The key to this success was that the names of the principal contributors were kept secret. This secrecy was crucial to the success of the antisaloon campaign, and as Warburton (1932, 263) notes, statistical investigations have provided little support for determining the *extent* of commercial rent seeking against the alcohol industry.

It is known that A. I. Root of the Root Beer Company made substantial contributions during the formation of the league. John D. Rockefeller admitted to contributing over $350,000 to the league, although unsubstantiated claims place that figure in the tens of millions of dollars. The Brewers' Association put forward a list of "known" contributors, which included officers of Roger Peet and Company, several owners of motor car companies, James Horton of the Horton Ice Cream Company, the U.S. Steel Corporation, John Wanamaker, and several prominent officers of major corporations. Owners and operators of such companies as Coca-Cola and Welch's Grape Juice, which could expect to benefit from prohibition, were also suspected of being heavy contributors to the cause (Odegard 1966, 271).

The Progressive Era and Prohibition

The Progressive Era represented an overhaul of American society. The combination of "progressive" thinking and World War I provided the ideal opportunity to enact national alcohol prohibition. The league provided both a clear objective (the end of the saloon) and the organization, so that a coalition of evangelical Protestants, women, professional organizations, and commercial interests could take advantage of this opportunity.[6]

---

[6]Professional organizations will be discussed at greater length later. Professional medical organizations were an important component in the drive for drug and alcohol prohibitions. For example, in 1914 a group of psychiatrists and neurologists condemned alcohol as a "definite poison" and urged state legislatures to ban its use. In 1915 whiskey and brandy were removed from the United States Pharmacopoeia as a medicinal drug. In 1918 the American Medical Association (AMA) unanimously passed a resolution which called for an end of the use of alcohol as a beverage and urged that its use as a therapeutic agent be further discouraged. At that same convention of the AMA, its president, Dr. Charles H. Mayo, expressed support for a national prohibition on the use of alcohol (Timberlake 1963, 47).

American society changed in many important respects during the Progressive Era. In political matters, the initiative, referendum, recall, direct election of senators, woman suffrage, and adoption of the Australian ballot and shortened ballot were both goals of the majority and means of achieving other Progressive reforms. Many of these changes promoted the prohibitionist cause. For example, James Bryce (1910, 49) notes that the Australian ballot placed illiterate and immigrant voters (who generally opposed prohibition) at a considerable disadvantage because they now had to be able to read the ballot. In addition, alien voting was outlawed, and registration requirements were established in many cities, both restricting the power of immigrants and enhancing the prohibitionist position.

A long list of economic reforms was passed during the Progressive Era. These reforms included child-labor laws, public-education laws, labor and labor-union legislation, immigration restrictions, money and banking reform (the Federal Reserve Act), antitrust policy, and the income tax.

The Progressive movement was based largely on the fears of middle- and upper-class citizens in a rapidly changing society. Big business was seen as a threat to the economic system and to social stability. The lower-class and immigrant populations were growing and congregating in the rapidly expanding urban areas. While Progressive policies were new to American government, they were largely the result of a conservatism and an attempt to fix society, enforce middle-class morality, and protect the old-stock American way of life. Timberlake (1963, 1) concludes that in order "to achieve these ends, the Progressive Movement embraced a wide variety of individual reforms, one of the more important and least understood of which was prohibition."

The scientific arguments for prohibition were based largely on studies of the effects of alcohol.[7] Important evidence that associated alcohol with crime, poverty, disease, broken homes, social vices, and other evils was gathered. The correlation established in these early studies transformed social science from a science which examined individual character based on free will to one which placed primary

---

[7]A survey of these scientific studies is provided by Timberlake (1963, 39–47). The weight of these studies helped prompt the AMA to take a strong stand against alcohol and to favor prohibition.

emphasis on the environment. According to Timberlake (1963, 60), "the chief effect of these sociological data was to persuade many people to turn to saloon suppression and prohibition" in order to improve the environment.

The saloon was the natural target of prohibition forces. It served a variety of functions for the poor, working, and immigrant classes. There they found comfort, entertainment, games, political discussion, job opportunities, and much more.[8] The saloonkeeper was the friend, confidant, and political leader of his regular customers. The reputation of the saloon became tarnished, however, through its association with widespread corruption, criminal activity, vote-buying, and monopoly power.

Saloonkeepers in several states often found it difficult to pay the annual license fees. One method of financing these fees was to have a brewer pay the fee in return for exclusive selling rights. Another method was to defy blue laws to generate additional revenues. Staying open for business on Sundays helped not only to pay the government fees but also to help retain the saloon's working-class customers who drank on Sundays.

To avoid the blue laws, bribes were paid to police and elected officials. These bribes came in the form of either money or votes. Another practice was to serve poor-quality or watered-down liquor as premium brands. Saloonkeepers also expanded their income with kickbacks from prostitutes, gamblers, and in a few instances pickpockets whom they allowed to use their facilities. Again the saloonkeeper protected himself by paying bribes to the local police and elected officials. According to Timberlake (1963, 110): "The liquor industry became thoroughly involved in political corruption through its connection with the saloon. The root of the trouble here was that the ordinary saloonkeeper, confronted by overcompetition, was practically forced to disobey the liquor laws and to ally himself with vice and crime in order to survive. Unable to make a living honestly, he did so dishonestly."

Prohibition forces focused on this crime-ridden industry that was

---

[8]Timberlake (1963, 118) provides a long list of services supplied by various saloons, including free food, card tables, exercise rooms, pool tables, and reading materials. The saloon was also the center of political life. "In short, [the saloon]was the poor man's, and hence the immigrant's, club par excellence."

capable of corrupting both the political leadership of the country and the lives of the poor immigrants. The success of National Alcohol Prohibition depended vitally on defining its goal as ridding America of the saloon. It should be noted, however, that high license fees, excise taxes, and other political requirements were responsible for this "overcompetition" and dishonest activity.

The alcohol industry had organized to protect itself from prohibition by establishing the United States Brewers' Association in 1862 and the National Retail Liquor Dealers' Association in 1893. Although it used its tremendous resources directly to affect elections and legislation, the alcohol industry was held accountable to the Corrupt Practices Act and suffered several election-law setbacks. These changes were partially responsible for the success of Prohibition. For example, the Australian ballot and other changes that occurred between 1890 and 1910 not only restricted immigrant voting but limited the alcohol industry's ability to influence elections by purchasing votes. Gary M. Anderson and Robert D. Tollison (1988) argue that the inability to allocate votes efficiently as a result of voter-secrecy laws causes instability in electoral outcomes and therefore contributes to the growth of government. The alcohol industry's political activities were further curtailed by an election-fraud conviction in Texas and an investigation in Pennsylvania that resulted in a million-dollar fine (Sait 1939, 149n.).

The coalition between the liquor interests and brewers broke down during World War I with the passage of the Lever Act. The act distinguished between hard liquor, which would be forbidden, and beer and wine, which would be restricted in order to free resources for the war effort. The beer industry tried to protect its interests by dissociating from the distillers: " 'The true relationship with beer,' insisted the United States Brewers' Association, 'is with light wines and soft drinks—not with hard liquors. . . .' The brewers affirmed their desire to 'sever, once and for all, the shackles that bound our wholesome productions . . . to ardent spirits. . . .' But this craven attitude would do the brewers no good" (Rothbard 1989, 86). Once the coalition was broken, prohibitionists turned their sights to the brewers, employing the anti-German sentiment and wartime patriotism provided by World War I to achieve their goals (Rothbard 1989).

A good deal of the political success of Prohibition can also be attributed to the fact that it attacked the saloon and did not include any injunction against the consumer of alcohol. Only the producers and distributors of the products were legally restricted. This tactic removed the personal-liberty argument, did not alienate the general population, and, most important, increased the isolation of the alcohol industry.[9]

The history of alcohol reveals several important components of the demand for prohibition that are consistent with the interest-group theory of the origins of prohibitionism. The basic demand for temperance is found in reform movements and evangelical postmillennial Protestantism. This temperance movement is then transformed into a prohibition movement through access to the political process. The prohibition movement develops and is joined by commercial rent seekers, such as competitors of the alcohol industry.[10]

NATIONAL NARCOTICS PROHIBITION

The national prohibition on narcotics was adopted before that on alcohol and has continued to the present day. This prohibition has several important factors in common with alcohol prohibition— evangelical Protestant and Progressive backing, the general impatience with progress in counteracting drug abuse, discrimination against minority immigrant groups, the unintended and unperceived consequences of government intervention, and the window of opportunity provided by World War I. Narcotics prohibition also had some important differences in the coalition that supported it. A primary difference was the role of the medical and pharmaceutical professions, which used narcotics control as a means of uniting and consolidating their professions into powerful interest groups. As David Musto notes, "Medicine and pharmacy were in active stages of professional organization when they became involved with the issue of narcotic control. . . . Their intense battles for professional

---

[9]The only support for the alcohol industry came from its bankers, and its own labor unions. Other industrial leaders supported Prohibition for either moral, economic, or self-interested reasons. Very little was made of the "rights" of the alcohol industry.

[10]It is widely acknowledged that many religions oppose alcohol and alcohol sales on Sundays because alcohol competes for the attention and money of church members.

advancement and unification had an effect on the progress and final form of antinarcotic legislation" (1987, 13). Politicians also took an active role in narcotics control. According to Arnold Taylor (1969) narcotics control was used to achieve influence in relations with China. And finally, bureaucrats helped to transform the regulatory role established by this coalition into a prohibition administered by a federal bureaucracy. An important reason for the longevity of narcotics prohibition is that consumers of narcotics, unlike alcohol consumers, have always been a small fraction of the population.

The Narcotics Problem

The raw materials for narcotics—opium and coca leaves—had been used for centuries in Asian and South American cultures before their introduction to America. Technological inventions and discoveries during the nineteenth century, such as morphine (1803), the hypodermic syringe, cocaine, chloral hydrate (1868), and heroin (1898), greatly increased the use and applicability of narcotics. Initially, these developments increased the prestige of the pharmaceutical industry and the medical profession's ability to cure diseases and alleviate pain. It should be remembered that the healing profession still relied on practices such as bloodletting, blistering, and mercury cures. It should also be noted that in addition to alleviating pain (aspirin was not commercially available until 1899), narcotics were valuable anesthetics and curatives. Courtwright (1982) cites the medical profession as the major source of opiate addiction.

In explaining the growth of narcotics addiction in America, authorities have often cited the Civil War. Many soldiers from both the North and South became addicts during the war. While many historians downplay the role of the Civil War, Courtwright (1982, 55) reports that 10,000,000 opium pills and 2,841,000 ounces of opium powders and tinctures were issued to the Union army alone. Statistics indicate, however, that consumption of opium was already on the increase in the 1840s.

The alcohol prohibition movement unwittingly played a significant role in the spread of opium addiction. The lack of supply of alcohol and the stigma attached to it no doubt encouraged the substitution of opiates that occurred in the middle of the nineteenth century. Dr. F. E. Oliver (1872) addressed this issue at great length:

The question how far the prohibition of alcoholic liquors has led to the substitution of opium, we do not propose to consider. It is a significant fact, however, that both in England and in this country, the total abstinence movement was almost immediately followed by an increased consumption of opium. In the five years after this movement began in England, the annual importations of this drug had more than doubled; and it was between 1840 and 1850, soon after teetotalism had become a fixed fact, that our own importations of opium swelled, says Dr. Calkins, in the ratio of 3.5 to 1, and when prices had become enhanced by fifty per cent "the habit of opium chewing," says Dr. Stille, "has become very prevalent in the British Islands, especially since the use of alcoholic drinks has been to so great an extent abandoned, under the influence of the fashion introduced by total abstinence societies, founded upon mere social expediency, and not upon that religious authority which enjoins temperance in all things, whether eating or drinking, whether in alcohol or in opium." And, in other countries, we find that where the heat of the climate or religious enactments restrict the use of alcohol, the inhabitants are led to seek stimulation in the use of opium. Morewood, also, in his comprehensive History of Inebriating Liquors, states that the general use of opium and other exhilarating substances, among the Mahometans, may date its origins from the mandate of the Prophet forbidding wine. These statements accord with the observations of several of our correspondents, who attribute the increasing use of opium to the difficulty of obtaining alcoholic drinks. It is a curious and interesting fact, on the other hand, that in Turkey, while the use of wine of late years has increased, that of opium has as certainly declined.

General economic progress also helped to bring the average American increasingly into contact with doctors, health-care facilities, and the multipurpose narcotic. It was also this progress that helped bring the problems of drug abuse and addiction to the attention of the general public after the Civil War: "The United States always had a 'drug problem,' though the public remained uninformed about it. But rapid communication eroded that ignorance after 1865. Like the railroad station and the courthouse, the sanitarium was becoming a monument to civilization" (Morgan 1974, 3). In fact, the term "addiction" was coined long after the Civil War by the Swedish doctor Magnus Huss (1807–90). The realization of narcotic addiction brought about efforts by doctors and patent-medicine companies to discover the cause, the cure, and methods to reduce abuse. Some progress was made in understanding the cause and cure of addiction, even by modern standards.

The Professional Movement

The American Medical Association (AMA), founded in 1847, and the American Pharmaceutical Association (APhA), founded in 1852, played important roles in the prohibition movement. They began as splinter groups within the medical and drug-dispensing industries. Their goals centered on the establishment of professional standards in order to restrict entry. This desire to implement standards initially aroused both suspicion and opposition from within their own ranks.

A common interest of the associations was the regulation of sellers of narcotics as a means of the advancement of the associates' economic goals and as a cure for growing social problems. Both associations also supported the call for alcohol prohibition. Another common interest was the destruction of an economic rival—the patent-drug industry.

The patent-drug industry had gained a substantial advantage over doctors and pharmacists as the result of improving technology, commercial practices, transportation, and communication. Patent medicines could be purchased anywhere by mail, while doctors and pharmacists were generally located in populated areas.

The AMA and the APhA were not completely united on policy matters. Indeed, much of the rent-seeking battles hinged on the competition between pharmacists and doctors who dispensed their own medicines. Despite this rivalry, Musto claims that "Physicians and pharmacists were vocal and effective in their lobbying efforts. Each saw that in addition to aiding the public welfare, strict narcotic laws could be a distinct advantage for institutional development if great care was exercised in their framing" (1987, 14).

The two professions were not the only two pressure groups involved in developing narcotics legislation. The National Drug Wholesalers Association, the Association of Retail Druggists, and other groups also participated. Public opinion was such that by the turn of the century it was not so much a matter of whether something should be done but rather what should be done, and more specifically how prohibition should be established. This situation provided a natural invitation for the medical and pharmaceutical industries to assist, as experts, in the development of antinarcotic legislation, and indeed the ultimate legislative outcome was largely determined by the interests of these groups.[11]

The Harrison Narcotics Act

The Harrison Narcotics Act was passed in 1914. It represents the first federal regulation to restrict the sale of drugs and is the basis of the current prohibition against narcotics. The Harrison Act represents the culmination of the haphazard work of a variety of interest groups joined against narcotics. According to Eldridge "The enactment of the Harrison Act marked an embarkation upon a totally new approach to the narcotics problem. That approach can best be described as an effort which set out to control the non-medical use of narcotics and evolved into the prohibition of non-medical uses and the control of medical uses" (1967, 9).

The first laws against the smoking of opium were passed in the western states. The use of opium was spread by the Chinese who migrated with the construction of railroads and used opium for a variety of medicinal and recreational purposes. The laws, often explicitly discriminatory against Chinese immigrants, were largely ineffective, because the Chinese formed close-knit social structures. In addition, there was no organized enforcement mechanism. To the extent these laws were effective, however, they tended to stimulate the use of less conspicuous forms of opium (that is, smokeless), the mail-order drug business, smuggling, and illicit opium dens.

Cocaine was viewed as a wonder drug and was used as an ingredient in a variety of commercial products, such as wine, Coca-Cola, and tonics. States began to ban the open sale of cocaine after 1900. In the South, cocaine prohibitions were in part based on the fear that blacks would substitute cocaine for alcohol after alcohol sales had been prohibited. It was claimed that cocaine use made blacks crazed criminals and violent rapists, as well as impervious to .32 caliber bullets.

---

[11]Estimates of the amount of narcotic addiction vary widely, but most early estimates put the population at 0.5 percent or less of the total population. See Courtwright (1982, 9–34) for an in-depth discussion and review of the evidence.

A major source of opiates was patent medicines. Only a small proportion of these products was consumed by persons who became addicted to them. Most patent medicine was used for pain relief and disease without addiction, or by babies who could not carry on a habit. Many addicts continued their addictions with patent medicines, while some unwittingly did so with opium-based addiction cures.

The real tragedy of the patent-medicine episode was the addiction of unsuspecting (and previously unaddicted) consumers. Many states banned opium, morphine, and heroin about the turn of the century, but the bans were largely ineffective for a variety of reasons. The most notable reason was that patent-medicine companies could readily obtain exemptions from the bans. These exemptions resulted in the widespread availability in unmarked form of a prohibited substance. The consequent addiction of many unsuspecting consumers can be attributed to state prohibitions and the exemptions granted rather than to the callousness or stupidity of patent-medicine companies.

The year 1906 was a watershed in the development of the national prohibition of narcotics. Media accounts of "abuse" by patent-medicine companies and the widespread failure of state bans helped promote a consensus on drug-abuse policy. The District of Columbia Pharmacy Act and the Pure Food and Drug Act were both passed in 1906 in order to halt the abuses by patent-drug companies and unlicensed competitors.

The Pure Food and Drug Act of 1906 was the first important piece of federal legislation directed at drug abuse. It mandated that patent-medicine companies list the ingredients of their products on the label. The result attributed to this legislation was the decline in sales of patent medicines.[12] The success of passing the act gave political experience and encouragement to the AMA, the APhA, and the wholesale-drug industry. The success of the law in limiting competition also encouraged them to increase their legislative efforts.

---

[12]At this time the general substitutability of intoxicants was again recognized. Dr. Hamilton Wright, the father of American narcotics laws, noted that in Prohibition states, opiate use had increased by 150 percent (Musto 1987, chap. 1, n. 42). Further, the decrease in opiate-based patent medicines (25–50%) might have been responsible for the notable increase in per-capita consumption of alcohol.

The Pharmacy Act was a trial balloon promulgated with the consent of the trade associations, physicians, and pharmacists. Indeed, the law was based on a model law, developed by the American Pharmaceutical Association, that exempted physicians who sold medicine to their own patients. This law had the effect of controlling competition from unlicensed (and unorganized) sellers of drugs, such as door-to-door salesmen. The final version of the law was a compromise between reformers, physicians, pharmacists, the drug industry, and Congress (Musto 1987, 21–22).

· The Spanish-American War had officially moved the United States into the ranks of the world's imperialist-colonial powers. Addiction and a newfound influence in the Far East brought narcotics use to a new level of importance. Western countries had used military power to open up the opium trade and to extend trading opportunities in China. The United States sought to increase its influence with China, lessen China's concern over the widespread discrimination against immigrant Chinese, and stop the source of its own drug problems by establishing international agreements on the control of narcotics.

Theodore Roosevelt promoted the Second Hague Peace Conference in order to establish an international agreement on the elimination of opium abuse. During the conference, in 1909, Congress quickly enacted a ban on the importation of smoking opium to relieve the embarrassment of the United States' delegation over a lack of federal laws of its own. This was the only legislation that would not offend the special-interest groups and could be quickly passed by Congress. This face-saving maneuver, however, did not achieve the original goals of Roosevelt or placate those interested in using that international forum as a method of imposing more restrictive domestic measures on narcotics use.

Continued attempts by the federal government (politicians) to gain influence in China and to control domestic narcotic sales led to the drafting of the Foster Anti-Narcotic Bill. Although it never passed Congress, the bill formed the basis of the Harrison Act. Based on the federal government's revenue powers, the bill was comprehensive and imposed heavy penalties on violators. The bill was to apply to all products containing even minute amounts of opiates, cocaine, chloral hydrate, or cannabis. It required that sellers keep extensive records, pay license fees, and purchase bonds and revenue stamps.

Penalties consisted of fines of $500 to $5,000 and imprisonment from one to five years.

The Foster bill was not popular with the drug interests because it placed the blame and the financial burden on pharmacists, physicians, and drug companies. Wholesale druggists and drug manufacturers attacked the inclusion of cannabis, the costly reporting requirements, and the severe penalties imposed by the bill. The American Pharmaceutical Association, social reformers, and bureaucrats wanted strong legislation, covering even cannabis and caffeine. Because of a lack of agreement between these groups, the Foster bill was eventually defeated (Musto 1987, 40–48).

The effort to control narcotics was placed in the hands of Congressman Francis Burton Harrison. In response, the American Pharmaceutical Association organized the National Drug Trade Conference, which consisted of the American Association of Pharmaceutical Chemists, the National Association of Medicinal Products, the National Association of Retail Druggists, and the National Wholesale Druggists' Association, all of which opposed aspects of a Foster-type bill.

In seeking a compromise between political and industry interests, Harrison squashed the influence of the reformers and bureaucrats. Harrison sought the direct counsel of the National Drug Trade Council in order to rewrite the Foster bill for passage. The American Medical Association had nearly quadrupled its membership from 1900 to 1913, and its interest was to obtain legislation which did not impinge on the rights of doctors to sell drugs. The pharmacists' lobby had long sought a monopoly on dispensing drugs. The sale of medicines by doctors was of decreasing importance, however, and the APhA was content with equal and less stringent record-keeping requirements. Musto described the final version of the Harrison Act as a series of compromises between the drug interests, the medical profession, reformers, and bureaucrats:

The descendant of the stricter Foster bill, the Harrison bill of 1913 had incorporated numerous compromises. Records were simplified; standard order blanks would be filled in by any purchaser of narcotics and kept for two years so that the revenue agents could inspect them at will. Physicians could dispense drugs without keeping records if in actual attendance on their patients. Numerous patent medicines containing no more than the permitted amounts of morphine, cocaine, opium, and heroin could continue to be sold by mail order and in general stores. Everyone dealing in narcotics except the consumer would have to be registered. Retail dealers or practicing physicians could obtain a tax stamp for one dollar a year. No bond was required, the drugs were not taxed by weight, and chloral hydrate and cannabis were omitted in the final version. (1987, 51–65)

In other words, the legislation gave pharmacists and doctors a carefully divided monopoly over the sale of narcotics, without offending related industries and without imposing much cost or burden on the monopolists themselves. At the same time, it did remove the influence, power, and control of bureaucrats, which was a notable feature of the Foster bill.

With the passage of the Harrison Act, the Bureau of Internal Revenue began to administer the new law. It had experience in collecting taxes, issuing revenue stamps, and registering participants. The bureau began to explore its authority and to answer practical questions of the law. It issued new regulations that placed increased burdens on sellers of narcotics and that conflicted with the interest groups' interpretation of the law. Second, and more important, was its assault on the maintenance of narcotic addicts.

The Bureau of Internal Revenue sought to eliminate addict maintenance by physicians, but these efforts were continually rebuffed by the courts. It was not until 1919 that the maintenance of addiction, and therefore strict prohibition of narcotics, was established. The prohibition was based on an amendment that strengthened the Harrison Act and on a favorable Supreme Court decision that upheld the elimination of maintenance programs.

The dramatic change in policy is linked to the enactment of (alcohol) Prohibition in 1919, the concerted efforts of bureaucrats, and events relating to World War I. The Prohibition amendment gave added authority to arguments for narcotics prohibition. It also established the fear that people deprived of alcohol would turn to narcotics. The Treasury Department's Special Committee on Narcotics produced a report, *Traffic in Narcotic Drugs*, in which questionable statistics (based on survey information) were used to paint a grim picture of future narcotics use in the absence of a total prohibition. In addition, World War I added fuel to the prohibition fires. Concern for efficiency, the Communist threat, and wartime patriotism helped to provide public support for measures that had been considered unconstitutional. As a result, the Narcotics Division of the Prohibition Unit of the Treasury Department was able to establish what was essentially a prohibition on narcotics.

In retrospect, the haphazard rent-seeking process that led to the current narcotics prohibition was not a sensible basis for legislation. Political influence in China, the promotion of medical-interest groups, Prohibition, and the initial problems associated with narcotics were one-time factors which no longer exist as support for prohibition.

NATIONAL MARIJUANA PROHIBITION

Prohibition seems incompatible with the historical, cultural, and economic significance of marijuana. As Ernest L. Abel notes, "Cannabis is undoubtedly one of the world's most remarkable plants. Virtually every part of it has been used and valued at one time or another. Its roots have been boiled to make medicine; its seeds have been eaten as food by both animals and men, been crushed to make industrial oils, and been thrown onto blazing fires to release the minute intoxicating cannabinoids within; the fibers along its stem have been prized above all other fibers because of their strength and durability; and its resin-laden leaves have been chewed, steeped in boiling water, or smoked as a medicine and an intoxicant" (1980, 269–70). Marijuana prohibition is also a curiosity because it was enacted before the use of marijuana as a recreational drug became widespread. These questions and the current importance of marijuana in the underground economy have led researchers to examine the origins of marijuana prohibition.

Two hypotheses have dominated the discussion of the origins of marijuana prohibition. The first is the "Anslinger hypothesis" developed by Howard Becker in the 1950s. Howard Becker (1963) argues that the Federal Narcotics Bureau, headed by the former Prohibition commissioner Harry Anslinger, played an entrepreneurial role in bringing marijuana to the attention of the general public. For example, Anslinger is responsible for developing the "killer weed" concept, and virtually all the popular articles published before the passage of the Marijuana Tax Act of 1937 acknowledge the help of his bureau and its publications.

Becker does not say the bureau sought this legislation, or why it did so at that time. Joel Fort (1969) argues that the bureau was seeking publicity, while Erich Goode (1972) maintains that the bureau was seeking to impose its own morality on society. Donald T. Dickson (1968) contends that the bureau was merely following its self-interest in the form of bureaucratic growth and survival of the budget cuts of the Great Depression. Jerome L. Himmelstein (1983) argues that the bureau was trying to sustain itself by limiting its responsibility and maintaining only a policy-setting role. All these hypotheses have some validity, although no single one, nor any combination of them, fully explains the origin of marijuana prohibition.

The "Mexican hypothesis," as developed by David F. Musto (1973) and John Helmer (1975), suggests that marijuana prohibition was a reaction against Mexican immigrants and others, such as blacks and lower-class urbanites. This hypothesis was based on spread of marijuana use to the general population during the 1920s and early 1930s, the presence of bigotry against the Mexicans, and the willingness of Mexicans to underbid whites in labor markets during the Great Depression.

It is evident that bigotry likely played an important role in the demand for prohibition. The Chinese, Germans, and Irish are prominent examples of discrimination through prohibition. From the evidence presented by Richard J. Bonnie and Charles Whitebread II (1974), it is clear that there was little widespread public concern with marijuana use in 1937, nor was there a public outcry for marijuana prohibition that was not linked in some way with the bureau or its publications.

The passage of the Marijuana Tax Act occurred without much publicity and did not become a significant policy until the recreational use of marijuana increased during the 1960s. The Anslinger hypothesis and the Mexican hypothesis are complementary; together they improve our understanding of the causes, justifications, and purposes of marijuana prohibition. At the same time, these two explanations appear to be incomplete answers to the question of the origins of marijuana prohibition. A more complete explanation may be achieved by placing the two competing hypotheses in historical context, with reference to the preceding prohibitions.

First, Anslinger was a commissioner of Prohibition during the National Alcohol Prohibition. When Prohibition was repealed, the

Great Depression was already creating budgetary pressure, and the Federal Narcotics Bureau required additional justification for its existence.

Anslinger had learned important lessons during Prohibition. First, bureaucracies that have difficulty in securing enough money to enforce their mission, are eventually exposed as ineffective. Second, Anslinger promoted the idea of punishing the consumer, as well as producers and distributors. He believed that Prohibition would have been effective had such penalties existed. Marijuana prohibition provided him with the opportunity to test his approach. Third, Anslinger was convinced that publicity and public support were crucial and that any means should be used to achieve this support.

In the Anslinger model of prohibition, a substantial majority should be pitted against a small and mistrusted minority. This would provide a stable level of public support and therefore continual funding for the bureaucracy. The federal bureaucracy should not be responsible for the actual enforcement of prohibition. Its role should be restricted to setting policy and to creating public support for the prohibition. With enforcement concentrated at the local level, problems and failures of enforcement would be less noticeable than at the national level.

Alcohol prohibition affected the market for marijuana. As the price of alcohol products increased during Prohibition, the relative price of marijuana fell and its consumption began to rise. It proved to be particularly popular with the lower-income classes who could not afford the high price of alcohol. Marijuana use spread more quickly in the Southwest and Midwest. It was also available in hashish form in several big-city speakeasies. Without the exposure that Prohibition provided, marijuana would likely have not become a matter of public concern or national legislation by 1937. In addition, the Harrison Narcotics Act of 1914 proved to be valuable for the bureau. Before the Harrison act, it was difficult for prohibition legislation to remain within constitutional guidelines. The precedent of using federal taxation powers and the experience of past court challenges to the Harrison act helped to establish the legality of marijuana prohibition.

This historical-theoretical perspective on the origins of marijuana prohibition achieves a comprehensive explanation that incorporates both the Anslinger and Mexican hypotheses. The Mexican (discrimination) hypothesis is valid in part. Most prohibitions involve an element of bigotry, and discrimination helps explain, for example, the decrease in penalties for marijuana during the 1970s, when middle-class white teenagers were arrested in large numbers for marijuana possession. The Anslinger (bureaucratic) hypothesis also helps explain the expansion of prohibition to marijuana and the manner in which it was executed. The historical and empirical implications of the two preceding prohibitions, however, are necessary to provide a consistent and complete account of the origins of marijuana prohibition.

The more traditional, rent-seeking explanation also contributes to our understanding of marijuana prohibition. Marijuana (hemp) has been one of the most important crops in human civilization. It was used extensively as a fiber, animal feed, medicine, oil, and in other ways throughout the world. By the twentieth century, substitutes such as petroleum and cotton had largely replaced hemp as the number-one source of these materials. Nevertheless, eliminating hemp as a substitute would be consistent with rent-seeking activity.

For example, the chemical industry and companies such as E. I. du Pont de Nemours that produced artificial fibers and petroleum-based drying oils (used in paints and shellac) would potentially benefit from the prohibition of marijuana. A prohibition against marijuana would provide chemical-based production and alternative natural sources of oils and fibers with an economic advantage. Despite the du Pont family's active involvement *against* alcohol prohibition, their company held a new patent on a process for wood pulp paper which would have had to compete against hemp-based paper had marijuana not been prohibited in 1937. See also Larry Sloman (1979) on the historical background of the marijuana issue.

Prohibition is a strange phenomenon, but no longer a mysterious one. Its origins can be found in the good intentions of evangelical Protestants and the discrimination against minority groups.[13] Politics offered the impatient members of the temperance movement a more

---

[13]Many of the progressive thinkers of the time were racists in the sense that they viewed the white race as superior and dominant and therefore responsible for the welfare of inferior races. Also see Warburton 1934 on the role of the Progressive thinkers.

direct and less costly method of achieving their goals—resulting in the loss of its voluntary and public-service nature.

Prohibitionism became an opportunistic special-interest movement joined in the public forum by a coalition of commercial-interest groups and professional organizations. While traditional rent seeking has been played down as an explanation for prohibitions, it was doubtless an important factor. Among the lasting effects of prohibitionism is the establishment of powerful medical interest groups. The American Medical Association became the dominating force during the drive for prohibition. Their monopoly power allowed them to close medical schools, control the remaining schools, and limit new entry. A major segment of doctors (homeopaths who used less expensive means of treatment) were shut out of the industry. Rubin A. Kessel (1958, 1970, 1972, 1974) describes some of the negative consequences that have resulted from the establishment of this monopoly. Burrow (1977) and John B. Blake (1970) also show that the medical and pharmaceutical organization gained control over the medical industry through licensing requirements and control over drug dispensing during the drive for prohibition. The organization, or monopolization of medicine has had important ramifications for health, innovation, price competition, and income distribution.

One of the most important conclusions of this study is that prohibitions were not enacted on previously unregulated products but on products that had already been subjected to massive government intervention. The worst problems with alcohol, such as those associated with inns and saloons, or in the case of narcotics, patent medicines, were actually the unintended consequences of interventionist measures, not the free market.

It was found that bureaucracies, once established, promoted and extended the policy of prohibition. This was especially true with narcotics prohibition and the prohibition of marijuana. Wars (Revolutionary, 1812, Civil, Spanish-American, and particularly World War I) were also shown to encourage the consumption of alcohol and narcotics and to play a major role in the establishment of prohibitions.

3

A Theory of Prohibition

The historical, biological, and statistical sources, however,
yield little in the way of verifiable facts or properly constructed data. The conclusions typically drawn after a reading
of this literature vary about as widely as the alleged facts and
are frequently derived without the aid of elementary logic.
—Robert J. Michaels, "The Market for Heroin before and
after Legalization"

Despite the heated debate little progress has been made toward a
theoretical understanding of prohibition. Economists and
other social scientists have spent much more effort on empirical
investigations and cost-benefit analyses than on theory. Historical
experience has added somewhat to our understanding, but only at the
cost of decades of misguided public policy.

Legal prohibitions are legislative acts which forbid the production, exchange, and consumption of a product. To provide a solid
foundation of understanding from which particular events and historical episodes can be studied, and as a basis for the formulation of
public policy and law, where permanence rather than transience is
desired, a theory of prohibition should remain general. It should not
refer to a particular product, whether "addictive" or not, or a particular time, any more than a theory of price controls or inflation should
do so.

In chapter 2, rent-seeking interests were discovered to be the key
element in the adoption of prohibitions. To establish the argument for
prohibition, these interests will be assumed to coincide with the public interest.

The arguments in favor of prohibition include:

1. Expenditures formerly made on prohibited goods would be put to better use on items such as life insurance, food, shelter, and savings.
2. Sobriety of the worker increases efficiency, reduces absenteeism, and reduces work-related accidents.
3. Consumption of prohibited products causes harm to the health of the consumer. Illness reduces time on the job, increases the demands on health-care facilities, and increases the cost of government-provided health care.
4. Addiction, compulsive behavior, and habits are problems beyond individual control and must therefore be placed in the control of the state.
5. Use of certain products causes violence and criminality in individuals who otherwise would not indulge in such behavior. Prohibitions help reduce crime, corruption, and social vices.
6. Use of certain products impairs education, family life, and participation in the democratic process. Therefore, prohibition is a way of defending the American way of life.
7. Use of certain products is infectious and would quickly spread to all socioeconomic groups, possibly leading to the addiction of substantial segments of the population.
8. Use of these drugs is unnecessary and has no beneficial social function.
9. Prohibition is the best possible policy available for the problems set forth above. It is effective, and the benefits of enforcing the policy far outweigh the costs.
10. Given a properly established policy with appropriate penalties and adequate resources, potential users will be discouraged from experimenting, and current users will be isolated or forced to abandon their habits. In the long run, then, prohibition can virtually abolish the product from the market.

The first eight statements offer plausible reasons for prohibition. Many of the expressed goals are laudable, but most would draw a great deal of disagreement.[1] Points 9 and 10 claim the superiority of prohibition over alternative policies and establish the necessary con-

---

[1] For example, point 3 offers the concern that consumption of certain products causes harm to the health of the consumer. According to a survey by the National Institute on Drug Abuse, however, the majority have considered

ditions for success. It is to these points that I address the following analysis. Ludwig von Mises described the economic approach of analyzing public policy:

> We are exclusively concerned with those acts of interference which aim at forcing the entrepreneurs and capitalists to employ the factors of production in a way different from what they would have done if they merely obeyed the dictates of the market. In doing this, we do not raise the question of whether such interference is good or bad from any preconceived point of view. We merely ask whether or not it can attain those ends which those advocating and resorting to it are trying to attain. ([1949] 1977, 734)

Before analysis, it is no more the job of economists to argue with government dictates than it would be for them to argue with the tastes and preferences of consumers. Rather, it is the job of the economist to analyze policy and determine its ability to achieve intended goals.

THE BASIC ANALYTICS OF PROHIBITION

Prohibition is designed to curtail the production, exchange, and consumption of a good with the ultimate goal of extinguishing it. While prohibition is an unusual and extreme form of government intervention, its effects can be analyzed within the framework of other interventionist polices such as taxation or regulation.

Penalties such as fines, confiscation of assets, and jail terms are established to discourage activity in the market. Enforcement of prohibition requires the use of resources to make the penalties effective in discouraging these activities. The diversion of existing enforcement facilities may involve some savings but does not eliminate the need for additional resources. The amount of resources devoted to the enforcement of prohibition will (with a given penalty structure) determine the degree of risk placed on market participants and therefore the effects prohibition will have on production and consumption.

---

only the consumption of heroin and the daily consumption of LSD, cocaine, amphetamines, barbiturates, or five alcoholic drinks to be harmful. In no case did more than 90 percent of those surveyed find the consumption of these drug products of great risk for harm to the user.

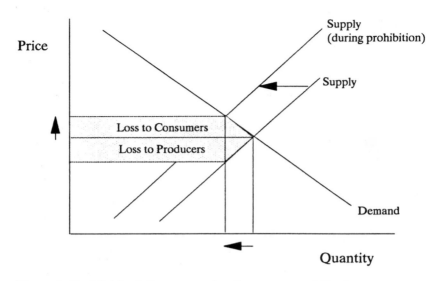

Figure 1. Prohibition's Impact on the Consumer and Producer.

Prohibition is a supply-reduction policy. Its effect is felt by making it more difficult for producers to supply a particular product to market. Prohibition has little impact on *demand* because it does not change tastes or incomes of the consumers directly. As supply is decreased, however, the price of the product will rise, the *quantity demanded* will fall, and demand will shift to close substitutes. For example, consumers of narcotics might shift their demand to alcohol and tranquilizers as their prices become lower in relation to narcotics as a result of prohibition.

The direct consequence of prohibition is to harm the consumers and producers of the product. The consumers lose utility because of the higher price and the substitution of goods of lower value. Producers lose income and utility by accepting occupations which differ from those dictated by their comparative advantage. These results are shown on figure 1.

As resources are allocated to enforcement, and prohibition becomes effective, the supply of the product is reduced (shifts to the left). Consumers are now worse off as a result of higher prices, loss of consumer surplus, and the substitution of lower-valued substitutes. Producers are likewise worse off as they suffer from increased production costs and risks, or from the transition to less desirable occupations.

The ultimate goal of prohibition is to eliminate supply of the good. It is difficult to imagine this result without fundamental changes in the "American way of life" that prohibition is designed to preserve. As a practical matter, an optimal, or cost-effective level of enforcement, rather than complete enforcement, is sought.

Efficiency in economics is the search to equate the marginal cost of an activity with its marginal benefit. For the individual, this means that the number of apples consumed depends on each apple's being valued at more than its cost. In public policy the situation is more problematic.

In simple terms, the marginal cost of prohibiting one unit of a product is the cost of the law enforcement necessary to bring about this result. Every dollar spent on prohibition enforcement means one less dollar that can be spent on alternative public policies such as national defense, shelters for the homeless, or Congressional postal privileges. If taxes are increased to fund prohibition enforcement, individuals will have less to spend on food, medical insurance, and lottery tickets. Initially, the declaration of prohibition, the use of excess law-enforcement capacity, and the existence of marginal users make expenditures on prohibition enforcement highly productive. Also, these resources can be diverted away from the least important policies or consumer expenditures and therefore can be obtained at a low cost. After these initial conditions, the price of additional enforcement increases, its productivity declines, and the cost of expended resources increases. The marginal cost of increased prohibition is therefore increasing, as illustrated in figure 2.

Disregarding the losses to consumers, the benefits of prohibition can also be generalized. The value of the first unit of a good is of the highest value. Additional units provide an individual with decreasing levels of satisfaction (utility). This *law of decreasing marginal utility* is a basic economic proposition on which this description of the benefits of prohibition is based.[2]

---

[2]When the losses to consumers and producers are disregarded this is a reasonably accurate description. Prohibitionists, such as Irving Fisher, often *claim*, however, that the marginal benefits of enforcing prohibition actually increase. This inconsistency of stated (rather than demonstrated) preferences is

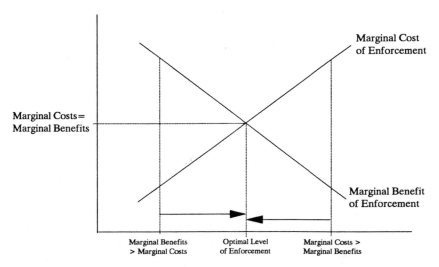

Level of Prohibition Enforcement

Figure 2. The Traditional Approach for Determining the Optimal Level Prohibition Enforcement.

The policymaker must find the optimal level of enforcement by determining the benefits provided by enforcement (in deterring production and consumption of the prohibited product) and the costs of this effort (which at present are limited to the direct costs of enforcement). By using the "traditional approach" described above to make these determinations, one can clarify the relationship between the cost of law enforcement and the price and quantity of the prohibited product. The results explain why prohibitions are never fully enforced in democratic nations—the costs of total enforcement far outweigh the benefits.

The traditional approach to policy based on the preceding analysis focuses attention on setting optimal levels of enforcement and determining the proper type and administration of enforcement. The

also revealed in an ABC News public-opinion poll, which indicates that most Americans favor spending "as much money as necessary to stop the flow of drugs into this country" and that most realize that "drug abuse will never be stopped because a large number of Americans will continue to want drugs" (ABC News, New York, May 8–13, 1985).

approach also balances expenditures between enforcement and demand-reduction policies, such as drug education.

Much more has become known about prohibition through decades of painful and costly experience. For example, one notable observation is that drug addicts will sometimes resort to criminal activity to pay the high prices of prohibited products. The traditional approach is a static analysis that retains assumptions of neoclassical analysis, such as a homogeneous product of a given quality. This oversimplification places important limitations on the analysis. A more detailed theoretical knowledge of prohibition is provided by the Austrian, or market-process, approach to economics.

Market-Process Approach

The Austrian, or market-process, approach to economic analysis is best exemplified in the works of Mises ([1929] 1977, [1936] 1951, 1922, [1949] 1977), F. A. Hayek (1937, 1945), and Israel M. Kirzner (1973, 1985). It begins with the truism that human action is purposeful and aimed at enhancing individual utility amid uncertainty and imperfect knowledge. Economic development occurs through exchange, learning, entrepreneurship, innovation, and the evolution of institutions. The market economy generates solutions to social problems; for example, the introduction (or evolution) of money reduces the transaction costs of exchange. The generation of such solutions is a discovery process because it requires alertness to opportunities and interaction between numerous individuals over time.

The market-process approach employs a multidimensional view of competition, whereas orthodox economists often rely on simplifying assumptions, such as homogeneous products. The market-process approach reminds us that goods are subjectively evaluated by individuals, who base their evaluations on many features of products. For example, a car is evaluated on the basis of age, design, style, color, size, power, materials used, fuel efficiency, and reliability, and many of these categories have multiple dimensions. The market produces a variety of products—determined largely by subjective choices from among the available technological possibilities.

This elaboration of the capitalist process indicates that entrepreneurs do more than drive prices to equilibrium levels. The entrepreneurial search for profits results in a competition based not only on price but also on alterations of the product and the development of new products. The market-process approach views disturbances of equilibrium as entrepreneurial moves to create new products and markets, to enhance products or information about the product, or to reduce cost. For example, one key element of the market process and economic development is advertising.[3] Advertising increases knowledge of a product, allowing the consumer to make better decisions while reducing search costs.[4] Advertising also assists in the development and introduction of new products and products with new characteristics.

Elements of the market–process approach have been integrated into modern economic orthodoxy. An important aspect of this integration is the "modern microeconomic synthesis," in which market-process elements have been synthesized with the neoclassical paradigm. A notable contribution in this area was by Lancaster (1966). His "new approach to consumer behavior" improved the understanding of product differentiation, complements and substitutes, advertising, and many other aspects of economic analysis that had become the "black holes" of the neoclassical paradigm.[5]

This new approach begins with the notion that economic goods consist of attributes and that these attributes (not the goods themselves) are what provide utility to users. Attributes of goods can be altered so as to enhance the utility derived from goods. The supply and demand for attributes follow the normal economic laws, and over time provide utility enhancement for the consumer (given free entry).

---

[3] Advertising is also a good example of the distinction between the Austrian-subjectivist approach to the market process and the neoclassical approach to markets. Austrian economists view advertising as an important, beneficial, indeed, crucial element in the market process. From a neoclassical viewpoint, however, advertising is inherently redundant, wasteful, and a tool to manipulate the consumer. The modern orthodoxy seems to have sided with the Austrian approach. On some of these issues see Hayek 1961 and Robert B. Ekelund and David S. Saurman 1988.

[4] Even "deceptive" advertising can convey knowledge of products and enhance consumer awareness. See Ekelund and Saurman 1988.

[5] Lancaster's analysis does not completely close the gap between process-oriented and orthodox neoclassical economists. His framework is static in nature, and value is objectively determined.

Interventionism and the Market Process

Interventionism is an alternative form of economic organization to capitalism or socialism, a form that involves governmental control or direction of resources that were private property. This popular form of organization includes price controls and regulations that are known to impose heavy direct costs on the economy, such as short-ages and surpluses, inefficiency, and waste. Prohibition is an extreme form of government intervention that has important implications on the entrepreneurial discovery process.

In addition to the direct effects of interventionism, economists have discovered important "unintended consequences" of interventions, such as the racial discrimination that results from minimum-wage laws. The costs of these unintended consequences have often been found to be greater than either the direct costs of intervention-ism or the perceived benefits derived from the intervention. Policymakers and orthodox economists do not anticipate (theoretically) these unintended and undesirable consequences because they are unaware of the causal relationship between interventionism and these effects, or simply deny the existence of such relationships.[6]

These consequences are predictable when the market–process approach is used to model interventionism. While all unintended consequences cannot be predicted in detail, they can be categorized in a way suggested by Kirzner (1985). Kirzner's four categories of results can be profitably applied to the policy of prohibition. As an extreme form of interventionism, prohibition can be expected to have more pronounced effects than other forms of intervention, such as regulation or price controls.

The Undiscovered Discovery Process

The undiscovered discovery process refers to the market's igno-rance or impatience with the progress toward solutions. It is difficult to imagine political solutions, however, without market discovery. Car safety features and nonsmoking sections in restaurants, for

---

[6]Policymakers may be unconcerned with unintended consequences, unaware of their possibility, or unaware of the connection between interven-tionist policies and the resulting unintended consequences. Economists may know of the existence of these results, but they often fail to incorporate these consequences into policy analysis and recommendations.

example, could not be mandated unless the market had first discovered them.

The demand for interventionist policies such as prohibition arises from the perception that the market process has caused an inefficient outcome or that the market will not correct inefficiencies. It may also be the result of the perception that the market should correct inefficiencies in a "perfect," instantaneous, and complete fashion.

The market's tendency for correction takes place under conditions of imperfect knowledge. Corrections take time, may not be immediately recognized, and are never complete in a world where equilibrium is never actually achieved. In other words, the market corrects for inefficiencies in an efficient manner, that is, resources are directed away from the least-valued uses toward the most highly valued applications. As Hayek (1945) has demonstrated, information in the market is dispersed and the policymaker can hope to gather only a small fraction of the vast amount of relevant information that exists. In contrast, the market uses all this information.

As shown earlier, prohibitions were often preceded by long periods of government intervention, rather than a pure market process. Prohibition was imposed because the harms of the prior intervention and the benefits of voluntary, market-based measures were not understood.

The market's discovery process results in less expensive, higher quality, and safer products. Prohibition terminates the discovery process and replaces it with a black market and a bureaucratic process, each with its own evils.

The Unsimulated Discovery Process

Prohibition establishes bureaucracy not to intervene in the market but to replace it. Government direction of economic activity is inherently different from the market process. Whereas market activity (production) takes place in a competitive, profit-directed environment, government direction (prohibition enforcement) is carried out in a bureaucratic, rule-guided environment. Entrepreneurs are motivated and directed by profits; bureaucrats are directed by rules and are precluded from receiving profits.

The general inefficiency of bureaucracy is well known and unavoidable. Because they lack incentives to do so, bureaucrats do not minimize the costs of production. William Niskanen (1971) found that bureaucracies could behave like monopolies because of their informational advantage over politicians. Bureaucracies themselves provide most of the information on which elected representatives base their votes on budgetary requests. Stigler (1977) found that bureaucracies were captured by the interests of regulated industries. C. M. Lindsey (1976) found that bureaucracies moved production out of desired activities and into observable activities. Bureaucrats find it to their (budgetary) advantage to allocate resources to produce "noticeable" results rather than uncountable, but more valuable, services. Even in the unlikely event that none of these incentive problems were present, bureaucracies would still face the information problems described by Mises ([1944] 1969).

Businesses are spurred on to implement new production methods, cost-cutting techniques, product enhancements, and new services in order to avoid losses and achieve profits. The discovery process is made easier because the market consists of many entrepreneurs who develop innovations that are generally recognizable and readily copied.

The bureaucrat has no such luxury. Bureaus are centrally directed and guided by rules; they have little access to innovations from outside sources. There is no systematic process that would result in less efficient bureaucrats being replaced or efficient bureaucrats being promoted, even if bureaucrats are assumed to be well intentioned. In fact, the Peter Principle suggests the opposite—bureaucrats rise to the highest level of their incompetence. Further, there is little scope for encouraging discovery by bureaucrats or for rewarding bureaucrats for discovery.

Thus bureaucracies cannot simulate the discovery, or successes, of the market. They have no way of knowing what the market would do in given circumstances and little incentive to find out. The lack of incentives results in less discovery of cost-cutting techniques and production techniques. In fact, successful bureaucracies often find their budgets cut, and innovative bureaucrats are often chastised, demoted, or dismissed. For example, two of the most successful Prohibition agents, Izzy Einstein and Moe Smith, were dismissed for doing their jobs in an honest and effective manner. "The two of them had raided three thousand speakeasies and arrested 4,900 people. They had confiscated five million bottles of bootleg liquor and smashed hundreds of stills. In every household from coast to coast Izzy and Moe were living proof that prohibition agents could be honest and incorruptible. But to be famous for honesty might seem an empty accomplishment when it was rewarded by dismissal" (Coffey, 1975).

The Stifled Discovery Process

Not only are bureaucracies incapable of discovery, they also stifle the discovery process of the market. Prohibition completely ends the discovery process of the market with respect to the outlawed good.

Some direct effects of government intervention are well known. Rent controls lead to housing shortages; minimum-wage laws cause unemployment. These results can be viewed on supply-and-demand diagrams, but these basic effects are not the only costs of government intervention.

In addition, intervention also discourages the development of new techniques, products, product characteristics, safety features, and sources of supply. These are the very types of discoveries that, given time, would make the call for intervention unnecessary, but which cannot take place because of the intervention.

Although we cannot know the magnitude of these stifled opportunities, they are costs of the intervention. In the case of prohibition, this cost is significant because the discovery process of the market is not merely stifled but destroyed altogether for the good in question and is severely curtailed or distorted for related goods.

The Wholly Superfluous Discovery Process

The elimination or control of a particular economic activity produces profit opportunities that previously did not exist. These profit opportunities will likely disrupt the plans of bureaus and undercut the pursuits of regulators and government policymakers. The severity of the intervention will determine the extent of these new (black-market) profit opportunities. Therefore, the wholly superfluous discovery process is particularly relevant to prohibition.

The profit opportunities created by prohibition will result in new methods of production, transportation, inventory, distribution, and marketing. The product, its quality, and attributes will experience tremendous change moving from a competitive market environment to one dominated by prohibition. These changes should of course be attributed to intervention, not to the market. Cave and Reuter (1988) found that entrepreneurs (smugglers) learn from experience; such increased knowledge can result in lower prices even during periods of increased enforcement efforts.

Bureaucrats are also subject to this wholly superfluous discovery process. Bureaucrats are normally unable legally to reap profit opportunities as residual claimants of their bureaucracies. Profit opportunities created by prohibitions, however, can be extended to bureaucrats by black marketeers in return for protection or selective enforcement. Bribery and corruption are unintended but nonetheless expected results of government intervention. Again, because prohibition is an extreme form of government intervention, corruption due to prohibition will occur to a greater extent than corruption associated with a price control or regulation.

In order to compare the severity of prohibition with other interventions, imagine a milk–price support established at $150 per gallon. Even at current levels, the milk price support program entices new suppliers of milk into the market. It encourages the development of special dairy cows, the use of special hormones and chemicals, and expensive feeding techniques. Even small amounts of smuggling and corruption can be detected. At a support level of $150 per gallon, one can imagine that missiles containing dried milk might be shot into the United States, that artificial forms of milk would be produced in basement chemistry laboratories, and that economists would become dairy farmers.

In summary, prohibition is advocated on the basis of misconceptions of the market's ability to solve social problems (although rent seeking is typically required for prohibitions to be enacted, as shown in chapter 2). Bureaucracies established by prohibition are inherently inefficient and unable to discover the knowledge required to solve social problems. Prohibition also suppresses the market's ability to solve social problems, so that little or no progress is made while prohibitions are in effect. And finally, prohibitions create profit opportunities which add to the problems prohibition is intended to solve.[7]

---

[7] I will apply this theory primarily to the prohibitions against drugs and the prohibition of alcohol during the 1920s. These results are, however, equally applicable to the prohibition of other goods, such as books, pornography, prostitution, gambling, etc.

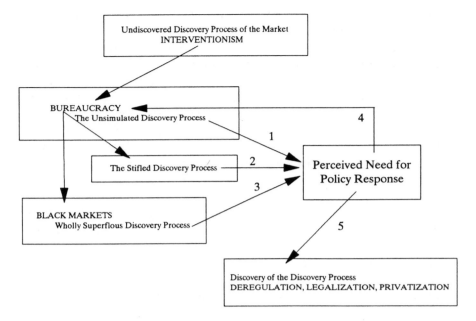

Figure 3. The Process of Progressive Interventionism (and exit).

THE POLITICAL ECONOMY AND PROHIBITION

The general tendency for one act of government intervention to lead to further acts of intervention has been modeled by James M. Buchanan and Gordon Tullock (1965). More recently, Bruce L. Benson (1984) has pointed out that each change in property rights establishes a new set of rent-seeking (and defending) possibilities. The process of this "progressive" interventionism is described in figure 3. Here, the expansion of intervention occurs for three reasons. Bureaucracy is inherently inefficient at achieving the sought-after results of policy, and initial failure leads to the call for more resources and powers for the bureaucracy to carry out its mission (1). The market has been stifled and therefore is unable to address social problems (2). And the activities of the bureaucracy create distortions and new problems in the market which "necessitate" (in the minds of bureaucrats and policymakers) further intervention (3).

The connection between the perceived need for policy response and more interventionism (4) is based on the institutional-based incentives of bureaucrats, politicians, and voters. Bureaucrats seek to expand their influence and power in order better to accomplish their original duties. This tendency for bureaucracies to grow is not dependent on the bureaucrats' being either selfish or public spirited. In any case, the bureaucrats do not perceive "failure" as the result of their own inefficiency. They are also unlikely to blame their own bureaucracy for problems generated from the wholly superfluous discovery process. Politicians who are ultimately responsible for bureaus receive benefits from them, and they are unlikely to admit failure or engage in the costly and uncertain procedure of dismantling a bureaucracy. Voters will perceive easily recognizable gains from the application of bureaucratic solutions, but they will not see the total cost. Bureaucracies tend to set the price of their outputs below cost (usually zero), resulting in a gain to the voter and a loss to the taxpayer. One result of this pricing policy is long lines for government services and the perception that more government is required. In the case of prohibitions, there never are enough enforcement agents to stop the problem.

The process of progressive intervention can only be reversed (5) by the electorate's discovery of both the true cause of the problem (intervention) and an alternative solution (the market). Because of the extensive transition and realignment costs, it is unlikely that elected representatives will act to dismantle a prohibition without extensive public support. In the event of the repeal of an intervention, bureaucracies must be quickly and thoroughly disbanded; else they will likely "discover" some new rationale for their existence.

Progressive interventionism is a recurring theme in the literature of political economy. It is a theme in which the policy of prohibition is often cited as a critical illustration. F. A. Hayek, Ludwig von Mises, and James M. Buchanan have pointed out the pernicious effects of using political institutions to intervene in economic activity and personal liberty.

Hayek's classic *Road to Serfdom* ([1944] 1977) was a warning that government planning of the economy was a threat to basic freedoms and that the acceptance of planning would result in socialism and totalitarianism. He noted: "Because of the growing impatience with the slow advance of liberal policy, the just irritation with those who used liberal phraseology in defense of antisocial privileges, and the boundless ambition seemingly justified by the material improvements already achieved, it came to pass that toward the turn of the century the belief in the basic tenets of liberalism was more and more relinquished" (19). Prohibition was just one part of the acceptance of planning by the people, "because they have been convinced that it will produce great prosperity" (61). According to Hayek, the acceptance of planning and interventionism is a break with the rule of law, a primary condition for a well-functioning economy. Hayek (72–87 and elsewhere) has written that this same rule of law is the basis for maintaining other freedoms. He quotes Max Eastman, a one-time Socialist, concerning the connection between economic planning and "democratic freedoms": "He (Marx) is the one who informed us, looking backwards, that the evolution of private capitalism with its free market had been a precondition for the evolution of all our democratic freedoms. It never occurred to him, looking forward, that if this was so, these other freedoms might disappear with the abolition of the free market" (104–5).

In discussing the economic results of planning, interventionism, and "the close interdependence of all economic phenomena," Hayek raises an issue for which planners cannot supply an easy answer: how can planning be controlled or limited? He notes that the results of economic planning "make it difficult to stop planning just where we wish and that, once the free working of the market is impeded beyond a certain degree, the planner will be forced to extend his controls until they become all-comprehensive" (Hayek [1944] 1977, 105).

Another economist who stressed this important aspect of intervention was Ludwig von Mises. In dealing with the issue of interventionism, Mises stressed the important political consequences of direct interference with consumption as it relates to the prohibition of drugs:

Opium and morphine are certainly dangerous, habit-forming drugs. But once the principle is admitted that it is the duty of government to protect the individual against his own foolishness, no serious objections can be advanced against further encroachments. A good case could be made out in favor of the prohibition of alcohol and nicotine. And why limit the government's benevolent providence to the protection of the individual's body only? Is not the harm a man can inflict on his mind and soul even more disastrous than any bodily evils? Why not prevent him from reading bad books and seeing bad plays, from looking at bad paintings and statues and from hearing bad music? The mischief done by bad ideologies, surely, is much more pernicious, both for the individual and for the whole society, than that done by narcotic drugs.

These fears are not merely imaginary specters terrifying secluded doctrinaires. It is a fact that no paternal government, whether ancient or modern, ever shrank from regimenting its subjects' minds, beliefs, and opinions. If one abolishes man's freedom to determine his own consumption, one takes all freedoms away. The naive advocates of government interference with consumption delude themselves when they neglect what they disdainfully call the philosophical aspect of the problem. They unwittingly support the case of censorship, inquisition, religious intolerance, and the persecution of dissenters. (Mises [1949] 1977, 733–34)

Therefore, the consequences of prohibition include its direct effects, the unintended consequences, and the tendency for intervention to influence the philosophy, size, and scope of government.

This aspect of political economy has received attention recently by the Nobel laureate James M. Buchanan. He showed that individuals can restrict the behavior of others at low cost by using the democratic process. This method of resolving conflicts is, however, deceptive and dangerous. "The majoritarian institutions of modern democratic politics are exceedingly dangerous weapons to call upon in any attempts to reduce conflicts in areas of social interdependence. They are dangerous precisely because the institutions are democratic and open to all citizens on equal terms . . . [and] preferences are as likely to be imposed upon as imposed" (Buchanan 1986, 339). Buchanan goes on to discuss the economics of partitioning issues that involve the prohibition of various activities. He notes that whereas the majority may benefit from a prohibition, the minority may suffer greatly. The democratic system as a method of conflict resolution allows issues to be partitioned and freedom of consumption to be taken away. Nothing exists in the purely democratic system to stop this process once the Pandora's box has been opened. Buchanan states: "Let those who would use the political process to impose their preferences on the behavior of others be wary of the threat to their own liberties, as described in the possible components of their own behavior that may also be subjected to control and regulation. The apparent costlessness of restricting the liberties of others through politics is deceptive. The liberties of some cannot readily be restricted without limiting the liberties of all" (340).

Before turning to specific results of prohibition, it is worth noting that its implications are much wider than basic economic analysis reveals. It is not mere speculation or chance that the macropolitical implications described above go hand in hand with prohibition and that these consequences are greater than those generated within a prohibited market.

4

The Potency of Illegal Drugs

> Another factor contributing to increased health consequences
> of marijuana use is the increase in potency over the past several
> years.
> —The White House Drug Abuse Policy Office, *1984 National
> Strategy for Prevention of Drug Abuse and Drug Trafficking*

D rug prohibition establishes a wholly superfluous discovery
process with respect to the potency of illegal drugs. Black-
market entrepreneurs are spurred on by artificial, prohibition–created
profit opportunities in a similar fashion to entrepreneurs in a legal
market responding to profit opportunities. At one level, the entrepreneur supplies a profit-maximizing quantity of *the* product, in both
legal and illegal markets. On another level, the profit motive prompts
entrepreneurs to alter production techniques, product quality, and the
product itself.

Market forces lead to certain industry standards, such as twelve
ounces in a can of soda and four rolls of toilet paper per package. Each
product line in the market, whether breakfast cereals or light bulbs,
moves toward an efficient level of product diversification (heteroge-
neity), the lowest cost of production, and optimal quality levels for
the product. In the black market similar tendencies exist. In prohibited markets, however, consumers face fewer choices at any time, but
severe product variability over time.

The potency of narcotics, cocaine, alcohol, and marijuana
increased significantly after the enactment of prohibition. In the
United States during the past century, opium was virtually replaced
by morphine and, later, morphine by heroin. The original Coca–Cola

contained small concentrations of cocaine. Today cocaine is sold in the form of a high-potency powder or as concentrated nuggets called crack. During Prohibition consumption of beer plummeted, and consumption of distilled spirits and moonshine increased. The potency of marijuana increased several hundred percent after a "prohibitive" tax was enacted in 1937. Synthetic narcotics and combinations of drugs, such as "speedball" (heroin and cocaine) or "moonshot" (crack cocaine and PCP), have been introduced.

Since 1968 when Simon Rottenberg published his germinal article, "The Clandestine Distribution of Heroin: Its Discovery and Suppression," economists have investigated many aspects of illegal drug markets, including alcohol prohibition, the problem of addiction, and public policy toward addiction and black markets.[1] Rottenberg examined several hypotheses for changing potency but concluded that his analysis did not answer the question of changing potency. "It is like explaining why Falcon automobiles will be manufactured, as well as Continentals, but would not explain why the fraction of Falcons rises and the fraction of Continentals falls" (Rottenberg 1968, 83).

The question of potency remains unanswered and largely uninvestigated despite its implications for public policy, the effectiveness of law enforcement and addiction, and the health of illegal drug users. The questions of potency and product quality also have important implications for basic theoretical and empirical investigations of prohibition and other public policy. Crawford et al. (1988) and Reuter, Crawford, and Cave (1988) found (indirectly) that entrepreneurs switched to smuggling higher-potency drugs when faced with increased enforcement.

Higher potency reduces the overall effectiveness of law enforcement because it means that smaller quantities represent greater effective amounts of the product. Higher-potency drugs are thought to be more dangerous and produce a greater risk to the health of the user, but actually great variance in the potency of a product poses a greater

---

[1]Rottenberg's article contains no references to economists or economic journals. Much of the recent research on illegal drug markets contains corrections, improvements, and extensions of Rottenberg 1968. The modern literature has generally ignored the economic analysis and experience of National Alcohol Prohibition.

risk to the user. Higher-potency drugs are also thought to be more addictive. In the black market the potency of a product is not fixed, consumers have less information about potency and added ingredients, and the producers are not legally liable in the same sense as pharmaceutical companies. In a recent study on the relegalization of drugs, James Ostrowski (1989, 47) claims that 80 percent of the 3,000 deaths per year associated with heroin and cocaine are the result of the illegal nature of the market, not drug use per se. (See also National Institute on Drug Abuse 1981–84.)

What caused the tremendous increases in drug potency after prohibition? Exogenous technological changes and shifting consumer tastes might provide explanations. For example, in figure 4 the market for drugs has been divided into high-potency and low-potency submarkets. If a technological change occurs that decreases the costs of high-potency drugs, shifting the supply curve to the right, this shift would cause a decrease in price and an increase in the quantity demanded. The changes in the market for high potency would lead to a decrease in the demand for low potency. These events would explain also the type of result observed under prohibition.

Technological changes are typical after prohibitions are instituted, but the type of technological change that occurs is not new technology but a different implementation of existing technology (see A. D. Little 1967).

The experience of prohibition, particularly of National Alcohol Prohibition, seems to rule out changes in consumer tastes as a cause for the increased potency of drugs. Once Prohibition was repealed, the pre-Prohibition expenditure patterns for both high- and low-potency alcohol reemerged. It appears that the dramatic change in potency of prohibited drugs is directly related to prohibition itself. The decrease in average potency over time of legal drugs, such as caffeine, nicotine, and alcohol, reinforces this proposition (Ippolitio, Murphy, and Sant 1979).

The explanation of higher potency offered here depends crucially on the effect prohibition has on relative prices of the same drug of different potency, the relative prices of different drugs, and the incentive for innovation in new drug products. The penalty structure, the level of enforcement, and the incentives of law-enforcement officials will be examined as causes for higher-potency and more dangerous drugs.

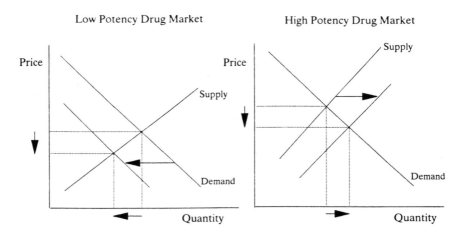

Figure 4. Effect of Improved Technology for High-Potency Drug Production.

THE ECONOMICS OF POTENCY

Lancaster's approach to consumer behavior (1966) provides a convenient structure for analyzing the economics of potency. This approach has helped solve many problems in neoclassical economics and has allowed economists to undertake the study of many new problems. The approach is based on the simple idea that goods are valued for their attributes, characteristics, or properties and are not the direct objects of utility. Economists have begun to investigate the composition of a good with the same zeal as physical scientists investigate the components of the atom.

Goods contain a variety of attributes that can be combined in a large number of finished products. Potency is but one attribute of drugs, representing the strength or concentration of the drug in its final form. Even a pure drug product would have additional attributes, such as coloring, taste, and freshness.

Each characteristic of a good represents an independent opportunity cost for the producer. Likewise, consumers evaluate each characteristic to determine the product's value and how much to buy. Therefore, for each attribute, supply and demand conditions exist; they may or may not be independent of other characteristics. While an enormous variety of products is possible, it would be inefficient for all possible products to exist at one time. The entrepreneur's job is to assemble attributes into a final product that maximizes profit.

Lancaster's approach helps answer two related questions in the realm of illegal drugs. First, what causes the tremendous increases in potency, and second, when all attributes are taken into account, what happens to overall quality?

Drugs have a number of characteristics that can be altered, and new characteristics can be added. Consumers demand the final products according to the value they place on the combination of attributes provided. The supply of products is based on the costs of producing a product with a particular combination of attributes, with each attribute having its particular cost. The products that survive in the market are those which provide the most efficient combination of attributes in relation to the costs of production.

PROHIBITION AS A TAX

Economists have drawn the analogy of taxation to represent the effects of prohibition. The enforcement of prohibition creates risk for suppliers of illegal products. This risk acts as a tax, thus increasing price and reducing output.

The theorem developed by Armen A. Alchian and William R. Allen (1964) provides a good example of how prohibition can affect the attributes of illegal drugs. In the original application of the theorem, constant transportation cost was applied to apples of various prices, resulting in a change in relative prices favoring the apples of higher price. More higher-priced apples are thus shipped out (table 3).[2] A similar change in relative prices should occur with prohibition if the prohibition "tax" is similar to a transportation charge or unit tax.

Yoram Barzel (1976) examined the effect of per-unit and ad valorem taxes on product attributes, after-tax price, and overall quality. His analysis indicated that depending on the type, taxation does affect the attribute composition of the product and therefore may be

---

[2]T. E. Borcherding and E. Silberberg (1978) found the Alchian and Allen theorem empirically reliable. They noted that the income effect could destroy most economic propositions. In prohibition the income effect strengthens the potency effect, and addicts attempt to hold income constant by resorting to criminal activities. Also see Gould and Segall 1968.

Table 3. Shipping the Good Apples to New York

	Price per Pound (Relative Prices)		
Grade	California	Transport Cost	New York
Choice	$.10 (2 to 1)	$.05	$.15 (1.5 to 1)
Standard	$.05 (0.5 to 1)	$.05	$.10 (.67 to 1)

Source: Alchian and Allen 1972, 71.

useful for understanding prohibition's influence on potency. A tax, depending on the type, results in a price and an output that differ from those predicted by the constant-quality model. According to Barzel, "Commodities as transacted in the market are complex, and the margins with respect to which optimization takes place are numerous. Because commodity tax statutes will not generally cover all these margins, any tax will induce multiple changes not only in resource allocation away from the taxed commodity and into others but also in the 'quality' of the commodity and how it is transacted, a substitution away from the taxed attributes and into the others" (1195). A per-unit tax imposed on commodity X containing n characteristics will induce inclusion of more of the untaxed characteristics. The commodity is defined by statute as containing a minimum amount of characteristics $1, \ldots, e$. The remaining characteristics, $e + 1, \ldots n$, are unconstrained by the tax. The imposition of the tax results in relatively more of the unconstrained-untaxed characteristics being included in commodity X. Quality upgrading and a higher-than-predicted price are the results (Barzel 1976, 1181). The per-unit tax, like the transportation cost for fresh food, induces quality upgrading.

An ad valorem tax imposed on a commodity with n characteristics has different results from both the constant-quality model and the constant per-unit tax. The tax would define the commodity as a minimum amount of characteristics $1, \ldots, e$. The ad valorem tax, however, would tax all the characteristics included in the product. Therefore, the inclusion of a characteristic and its level will depend crucially on whether it is cheaper to include the characteristic or to sell it separately to avoid the tax. The unconstrained attributes (those not defined in the statute) will be reduced, eliminated, or sold separately in order to avoid taxation. The product will sell for less than predicted by the constant-quality model and will result in a lower-quality product (of fewer characteristics). The ad valorem tax therefore reduces taxation by eliminating product characteristics in a way similar to that in which transportation charges eliminate characteristics. For example, fresh oranges and fresh orange juice can be considered higher-quality products than frozen or reconstituted orange juice. Suppliers of orange products, however, can greatly reduce the transportation "tax" on orange juice by shipping frozen concentrate, which is much less bulky than an equal amount of the fresh product. The frozen concentrate is then reconstituted with the addition of water and labor at the point of consumption.

Barzel found support for his hypothesis in the response of cigarette prices to changes in cigarette taxes. Excise taxes tended to increase the tar and nicotine level of cigarettes. Johnson (1978) provides additional evidence that ad valorem taxes result in lower prices and unit taxes result in higher prices than predicted by the traditional model of taxation. Harris (1980) also recognizes that increasing the per-unit taxes on cigarettes leads to a substitution of high-potency cigarettes for low-potency cigarettes. Sumner and Ward (1981) question the applicability of the evidence on cigarette prices by suggesting alternative explanations for diverging prices.

Feenstra (1988) found that the effect of a 25 percent ad valorem tariff on imported pickup trucks was ambiguous with respect to overall quality, while the import quota on Japanese automobiles led, as expected, to quality upgrading. These decisions are based on the cost of including a characteristic versus selling the characteristic separately. The ambiguous result from the ad valorem tax, however, is not unexpected in this particular case. Barzel (1976, 1183n.) notes that the price of the parts of an automobile was two and a half times the price of the same automobile assembled. In this example, the savings involved in purchasing an assembled car dwarf the effects of the 25 percent ad valorem tax. Japanese producers have also responded to the tax incentives by adding extra features to their "truck" products in order to get them classified as vans, which are subject to only a 2 percent tariff.

THE IMPACT OF PROHIBITION ON POTENCY

The type of taxation and the definition of the taxed commodity by the tax statute result in different effects on the quality and attributes contained in a product. The prohibition statutes and their enforcement play a similar role in determining product composition, quality, output, and price. The directives and incentives of law-enforcement officials will influence market outcomes such as product composition.

Prohibition establishes a gambling environment rather than an explicit tax. Participants who are actually caught face huge losses from lost revenue, fines, confiscations, and jail terms. Those not caught reap large monetary profits. All market participants, however, incur large costs of risk bearing. The tax is evaluated as a function of the penalties and the likelihood of capture and conviction.

Prohibition statutes generally consist of three parts. First, to be illegal, products must contain a minimum amount of a certain drug. During alcohol prohibition, products that contained more than 0.5 percent alcohol were illegal. A product containing any detectable amount of heroin is illegal. Second, penalties are generally levied on the basis of weight. For example, maximum penalties for marijuana possession in Indiana are a one-year prison sentence and a $5,000 fine for amounts up to thirty grams. The limits on penalties are doubled for amounts over thirty grams. Finally, penalties are established for production, distribution, and possession.

The prohibition statutes consistently define the product in terms of minimum potency (without constraining the maximum). Also, the heavier the shipment, the more severe the penalty. Since penalties are based on the weight of a shipment, suppliers will reduce the attributes that are not taxed when separated from the product.[3] Potency is unconstrained and will likely increase as suppliers raise the value of the shipment to reduce the relative burden of the tax. This aspect of prohibition statutes therefore acts as a constant per-unit tax.

In addition to the prohibition statutes, the probability of capture plays an important role in risk. The efficiency of law enforcement

---

[3]An example of such an attribute would be a substance used to reduce cocaine from a pure product to a potency that consumers would desire in the absence of prohibition. This is referred to as the "cut." This "cutting" of potency does take place but does so as the product proceeds to the ultimate consumer and the risk of capture and penalties decreases. The cutting may be done by several different individuals along the chain of distribution, and several different "cuts" may be used to adjust the potency.

relative to the size of the black market for drugs establishes (in part) the probability of capture. Suppliers of illegal drugs evaluate law enforcement and penalties to determine the risk they face and the allocation of their resources to avoid capture.

A key to avoiding capture is concealment of the shipment. While this can take many forms, the size of the shipment is a basic factor. Size is related to weight and will act as a constant per-unit tax, inducing a higher-than-market potency. Concealment efforts would increase at the margin as law-enforcement resources or efficiency increased. These factors therefore act to increase quality and result in a higher price than that predicted by the constant-quality model. Potency increases, and this increase is largely responsible for the increase in the overall "quality."

Prohibition may act like an ad valorem tax as a result of the directives of legislatures and the incentives of law-enforcement officials and judges. Lindsey (1976) showed that bureaucrats have the incentive to produce goods and services with attributes that are easily monitored and desired by Congress, while shirking the production of attributes that are not or cannot be monitored by Congress. For example, Lindsey found that whereas Veteran Administration hospitals produced measurable output (patient-days) at lower cost, proprietary hospitals provided more staff per patient, "better" physicians, shorter stays, less crowding and waiting, and more environmental amenities. Thus, in the same sense that taxation alters the attributes of products, the incentives of bureaucrats can alter the attributes of products.

With prohibition, the type of service provided by law-enforcement bureaucrats to Congress and state legislatures can have important effects on the mix of attributes in illegal drugs. One example of bureaucratic behavior is the technique of estimating the dollar value of drug confiscations. The value of drug confiscations is estimated using average "street price." The street price is the highest per-unit price because it represents the last step in product distribution. This estimation is akin to a farmer's ascertaining how much flour is required to make a loaf of bread and then multiplying the retail price of bread (per pound) by the total weight of his freshly cut wheat, including chaff, to determine the value of his crop.

Likewise, law-enforcement bureaucrats might view the capture of large or high-potency shipments as promoting their self-interest and satisfying the directives of the legislature. The capture of large shipments provides the bureaucracy with publicity about the effectiveness of their work and may help stimulate demand for their product (enforcing the drug laws). The concentration of law-enforcement resources on the interdiction of high-potency drugs would reduce the risk of shipping low-potency and less dangerous drugs such as marijuana and increase the risk of shipping high-potency and dangerous drugs such as heroin. Because the risk would increase so would their market value. This incentive would have an effect similar to that of either an ad valorem or ad potere (according to potency) tax.

Similar incentives may exist in the court system. High-potency shipments and more dangerous drugs may influence the probability of conviction. The court system has some discretion in determining penalties. According to current federal sentencing guidelines, higher-potency shipments may bring longer prison sentences and larger fines. The discretion of the court could therefore act as a constraining factor on potency and as an ad valorem tax.

The incentives of law enforcement and the court system, like ad valorem taxes, result in lower than expected quality and price, but do they constrain or reduce potency? Are these incentives—or ad valorem taxes—empirically relevant, as in Feenstra's (1988) examination of the import tax on Japanese pickup trucks?

Several points must be made about the existence or strength of the ad valorem effect on potency. First, it is likely that law-enforcement officials benefit more from capturing larger shipments that increase estimated street value than from higher-potency shipments that do not. Second, there is no reason to believe that law-enforcement officials have the means to discriminate between a high-potency and a low-potency shipment of a particular drug, except with respect to where in the chain of distribution it is confiscated. Third, while judges do have some sentencing discretion according to drug potency, this discretion is limited to interpreting the intent of the defendant within the penalty structure based on weight. Last, the pure ad valorem tax is not expected to have a marked effect on potency but rather a proportional effect on all product attributes.

Law enforcement may create an ad valorem tax in a multidrug illegal market. Concentration on more dangerous drugs such as heroin would have effects similar to those of an ad valorem tax on the entire illegal drug market, since the probability of capture from a unit of heroin would be greater than from a similar unit of marijuana. This aspect of prohibition enforcement does not constrain potency as a product attribute—it merely focuses greater resources and penalties on the more dangerous drug types. The expected results are similar to the situation of higher penalties for heroin relative to penalties for marijuana. We would expect that the higher penalties for heroin would result in higher potency relative to the increases in potency of marijuana, which is subject to lower penalties.

Many factors, such as the definition of illegal drugs, penalties based on weight, and probability of capture, do not constrain potency and therefore result in higher-potency drugs. Only the limited discretion of the courts was found to place a small constraint on potency. In a multiple illegal-drug market, differences in penalties and the incentives of law-enforcement bureaucrats intensify the effects of prohibition on heroin and reduce the effect on potency for drugs such as marijuana.

The evaluation of risk therefore places a strong incentive in increasing the potency of illegal drugs. Empirically, the cost of bearing the risk of prohibition is high relative to the cost of production and distribution in a legal environment. Edward Erickson (1969) estimated the prohibition tax on heroin at 20,000 percent. The cost of one ounce of marijuana is well over one hundred times the market price of an equal weight of cigarettes. Such high rates of taxation obviously have a major impact on the attribute mix of products.

POTENCY IN PROHIBITED MARKETS

The lack of reliable data concerning prohibited markets makes rigorous econometric testing impossible. Nonetheless, history provides several instructive illustrations concerning the potency of products in such markets. Two prominent episodes, Prohibition and the modern "war on drugs," are presented here.

These episodes provide enough information to present the correlations among prohibition, relative prices, and potency, as well as the correlations among changes in law-enforcement resources, relative prices, and potency. This information illustrates the product alteration and innovation that occurs during prohibition. In terms of

Table 4. Federal Expenditures upon the Enforcement of Prohibition
(thousands of dollars)

Year ending June 30	Bureau of Prohibition	Coast Guard	Indirect Cost	Total Cost	Fines and Penalties	Total Net Expenditures
1920	2,200	0	1,390	3,590	1,149	2,441
1921	6,350	0	5,658	12,008	4,571	7,437
1922	6,750	0	7,153	13,903	4,356	9,547
1923	8,500	0	10,298	18,798	5,095	13,703
1924	8,250	0	10,381	18,631	6,538	12,093
1925	10,012	13,407	11,075	34,494	5,873	28,621
1926	9,671	12,479	10,441	32,591	5,647	26,944
1927	11,993	13,959	11,482	37,434	5,162	32,272
1928	11,991	13,667	16,930	42,588	6,184	36,404
1929	12,402	14,123	16,839	43,364	5,474	37,890
1930	13,374	13,558	17,100	44,032	5,357	38,675
Total	101,493	81,193	118,747	301,433	55,406	246,027

Source: Warburton 1932, 246.

regression analysis, even these limited goals are difficult to establish because adequate data are simply not available. In these cases, using proxies for variables is like substituting Ping-Pong balls for turtle's eggs in a recipe.

ALCOHOL PROHIBITION

An examination of the prohibition on alcohol during the 1920s provides useful and interesting evidence on "shipping the hard liquor in." During Prohibition a variety of law-enforcement resources were mobilized through the Volstead Act in an attempt to curtail the production, sale, and consumption of alcohol. Enforcement created risks for alcohol suppliers, risks that had pervasive effects on how, when, where, and what kind of alcohol was consumed.

Table 4 provides information concerning the federal prohibition enforcement effort.[4] Total expenditures grew from less than four million dollars in the second half of 1920 to almost forty-five million in

---

[4]According to Warburton (1932, 247) no evidence exists which suggests that state and local governments spent larger sums during Prohibition than they spent formerly on regulatory or prohibitory laws.

1930. The annual budget of the Bureau of Prohibition doubled during this decade, with the greatest growth occurring between 1920 and 1925. In 1925 the Coast Guard's budget was augmented to enforce prohibition, doubling the resources devoted to interdiction and enforcement. The indirect cost, which included such expenditures as the costs of criminal prosecutions, also grew throughout the decade.

Fines, penalties, and net expenditures are not relevant for the purpose of determining law-enforcement resources. Fines and penalties do, however, provide some evidence of the effectiveness of law-enforcement resources. This effectiveness appears to have been weakened by the development of specialists in illegal production, the development of rigidities within the bureaucracy, and the corruption of public and law-enforcement officials.

Clark Warburton and Irving Fisher were opponents in the academic debate over Prohibition, but they both presented evidence concerning the dramatic change in relative prices that occurred during Prohibition. We would expect the change in relative prices to result from the risk imposed by law enforcement.

Warburton demonstrated that the price of spirits fell relative to the price of beer. Based on the average of four separate estimates of probable prices had National Prohibition not been enacted, the price ratio of spirits to beer would have been 15.42 to 1. The actual estimated ratio of retail prices in 1929–30 was 11.78 to 1, while the estimated cost ratio of homemade alcohol to homemade beer was 3.33 to 1 (Warburton 1932, 148–66). Estimates of full cost would lower these price ratios under Prohibition. Buyers faced the risk of confiscation, but this risk was lower for spirits because of its compact size.

As noted earlier, Irving Fisher was a major proponent of Prohibition. He used observations of increased prices to claim that Prohibition was drying up the supply of alcohol. Fisher used the data in table 5 to support his case. Calculations in parentheses are mine. Fisher's calculations to the right are of unknown origin. He did in fact show in his "alcohol price index" that alcohol increased in price. He also showed that lager beer increased in price by 700 percent while rye whiskey increased by only 312 percent, again supporting the case that the relative price of high-potency alcohol fell.

It is generally agreed that as a result of the increase in the price of

Table 5. Fisher's "Alcohol Price Index," 1916–1928

	Average Price per Quart		Increase in Price (%)
	1916	1928	
Lager beer	$0.10	$0.80	600 (700)
Home brew		0.60	
Rye whiskey	1.70	7.00	310 (312)
Corn whiskey	3.95		147
"White Mule" (bootleg whiskey)		3.20	100
Gin	0.95	5.90	520 (521)
Gin (synthetic)	3.65		285
Brandy	1.80	7.00	290 (289)
Port Wine	0.60	3.90	550 (550)
Sherry	0.60	4.32	600 (620)
Claret	0.80	3.00	200 (275)
Average percentage increase in alcohol price			360 (467)

Source: Fisher 1928, 91.

alcohol, the absolute quantity of alcohol purchased declined, a fact confirmed by Warburton. Consumption of high-potency-alcohol products, however, rose relative to low-potency-alcohol products, such as beer. The effect of lowering the relative price of spirits during Prohibition on expenditures and consumption is shown in table 6. Without explicitly making the connection to the change in relative prices, Warburton noted that "Prohibition has raised the amount spent for spirits to three and a half billion dollars, and reduced that for beer to less than a billion dollars" (1932, 170). Fisher was also aware of the "well known fact that Prohibition has been more effective in suppressing the drinking of beer than of whiskey" (1927, 29). T. Y. Hu, who lacked an understanding of relative prices, doubted this finding.

Prohibition's impact on consumption is further illustrated by placing it in historical perspective (table 7). Although alcohol consumption is related to various factors, such as income and alcohol taxes, certain trends are suggested. First, the consumption of beer increased during Prohibition, partly as a result of the decline in its relative cost of production and distribution. Second, total consumption of pure alcohol was more or less stable throughout the period.

Table 6. The Effect of Prohibition on Alcohol Expenditures
(millions of dollars)

Year	Probable Max. Expenditure without Prohibition			Estimated Actual Expenditure		
	Spirits	Beer	Ratio S:B	Spirits	Beer	Ratio S:B
1921	2,212	2,307	0.49	528	136	0.80
1922	2,245	2,069	0.52	2,704	188	0.93
1923	2,279	2,100	0.52	3,504	250	0.93
1924	2,313	2,131	0.52	3,168	321	0.84
1925	2,347	2,162	0.52	3,312	398	0.89
1926	2,381	2,193	0.51	3,568	490	0.88
1927	2,415	2,225	0.52	2,896	595	0.83
1928	2,449	2,256	0.52	3,360	726	0.82
1929	2,483	2,287	0.52	3,616	864	0.81
1930	2,516	2,318	0.52	2,624	850	0.76

Source: Warburton 1932, 170.

Third, expenditures declined before Prohibition because of increased taxation, wartime prohibitions, and state prohibitions.

Expenditures on alcohol as a percentage of national income declined by 2 percent from 1890 to 1910, more being spent on beer than spirits (55:45), a ratio that continued from 1911 to 1916 (Warburton 1932, 114–15). This pre-Prohibition consumption pattern was reestablished after the repeal of Prohibition, distilled spirits again accounting for only about half of all alcohol expenditures. During Prohibition (1922–30) expenditures for distilled spirits as a percentage of all alcohol expenditures grew to 70–87 percent. For the period 1939–60 distilled spirits accounted for 42–53 percent of total alcohol sales.

Did Prohibition lead to the innovation of new products that were highly potent and dangerous? Fisher's "alcohol price index" provides some evidence of this (table 5). Several new products, such as "White Mule" bootleg whiskey contained 50–100 percent more alcohol than the average market whiskey. Fisher noted that highly potent and dangerous products were responsible for distorting statistics, such as arrests for drunkenness. "I am credibly informed that a very conservative reckoning would set the poisonous effects of bootleg beverages as compared with medicinal liquors at ten to one;

Table 7. Per Capita Consumption of Alcoholic Beverages in Gallons, 1840–1919

Year	Spirits	Wines	Beer	Total Alcohol	Total Pure
1840	2.52	0.29	1.36	4.17	1.36
1850	2.23	0.27	1.58	4.08	1.22
1860	2.86	0.34	3.22	6.42	1.62
1870	2.07	0.32	5.31	7.70	1.31
1880	1.27	0.56	8.26	10.09	1.06
1890	1.39	0.46	13.57	15.42	1.34
1900	1.28	0.39	16.06	17.73	1.38
1901	1.31	0.36	15.95	17.62	1.38
1902	1.34	0.62	17.15	19.11	1.49
1903	1.43	0.47	17.64	19.54	1.53
1904	1.44	0.52	17.88	19.84	1.55
1905	1.41	0.41	17.99	19.81	1.53
1906	1.47	0.53	19.51	21.51	1.64
1907	1.58	0.65	20.53	22.76	1.75
1908	1.39	0.58	20.23	22.20	1.64
1909	1.32	0.67	19.04	21.03	1.56
1910	1.42	0.65	19.77	21.84	1.64
1911	1.46	0.67	20.69	22.82	1.70
1912	1.45	0.58	20.02	22.05	1.66
1913	1.51	0.56	20.72	22.79	1.71
1914	1.44	0.53	20.69	22.66	1.67
1915	1.26	0.33	18.40	19.99	1.46
1916	1.37	0.47	17.78	19.62	1.51
1917	1.62	0.41	18.17	20.20	1.64
1918	0.85	0.49	14.87	16.21	1.13
1919	0.77	0.51	8.00	9.28	0.80

Source: Johnson 1917, 321, and Warburton 1932, 24.

that is, it requires only a tenth as much bootleg liquor as of pre-prohibition liquor to produce a given degree of drunkenness. *The reason, of course, is that bootleg liquor is so concentrated and almost invariably contains other and more deadly poisons* than mere ethyl alcohol" (1927, 28–29, emphasis added). Friedman and Friedman (1984) also note that producers of these new products often used dangerous substitutes, such as wood or denatured alcohol, to increase the potency of the product: "Under Prohibition, both bootleggers and do-it-your-selfers producing bathtub gin sometimes used wood alcohol or other substances that made the product a *powerful poison*, leading to the injury and sometimes death of those who drank it" (140–41, emphasis added). Producers tended to practice poor distilling techniques and conducted little testing of the product. Adulteration is expected in prohibited markets because of a lack of a market for reputation, which Hayek (1948, 97) argues is necessary to ensure competition and contract performance. In addition to precluding recourse to negligence and liability law, prohibition also violates the conditions described by Klein and Leffler (1981) that ensure such performance and maintenance of quality in a pure market environment. With the consumption of alcohol declining, the increase in potency and the use of adulterants may indeed help explain why statistics on drunkenness and alcoholism did not also decline significantly during Prohibition.[5]

It is reasonably clear from evidence provided by both opponents and proponents of Prohibition that changes in relative prices were the result of Prohibition and these changes led to increased consumption of higher-potency drugs (spirits), as well as other higher-potency and dangerous products (moonshine).

THE PROHIBITION OF MARIJUANA: A SIMPLE TEST

The effect of prohibition on relative prices, potency, and consumption patterns of alcohol also applies to illegal drugs such as marijuana, cocaine, and heroin. Cannabis (marijuana) is an ancient crop, grown for commercial, medicinal, and recreational uses. Essentially it has been illegal since the Marijuana Tax Act of 1937. Marijuana became a major public-policy concern in the United States during the 1960s, when its recreational use increased significantly. In 1969, resources devoted to federal drug-law enforcement were expanded to curtail the importation and sale of illegal drugs such as marijuana and heroin. The commitment to prohibition has

---

[5]While the number of deaths per thousand due to cirrhosis of the liver did decline during the 1920s, it was declining prior to 1920. Changes in the age distribution (as a result of the men killed during World War I) and improvements in medical diagnostics and care also contributed to the decline. It should also be remembered that some people gave up alcohol altogether, so that the number of deaths due to cirrhosis and alcoholism per drinker was likely higher during Prohibition.

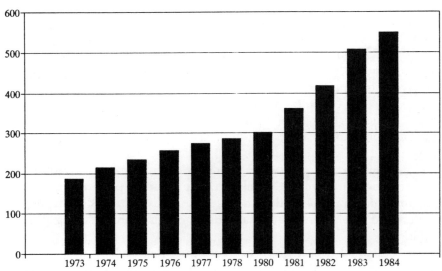

Source: Adapted from, The Budget of the United States Government: Appendix, U.S. Bureau of
The Budget, USGPO: Washington, D.C., 1973-1985 editions.

**Figure 5. Federal Budget for Enforcement of Drug Laws, 1973-1984
(millions of 1972 dollars).**

resulted in increased budgets for many federal agencies, such as Cus-
toms, Coast Guard, Drug Enforcement Administration, the Federal
Bureau of Investigation, and the Internal Revenue Service. The
combined budget of these agencies (attributable to drug-law
enforcement) is used to represent the federal law-enforcement effort
in figure 5.[6]

One effect of more intense law-enforcement effort is to increase
the risk of supplying illegal drugs. A price-theoretic model based on

---

[6]State and local enforcement of drug laws is an important consideration for
which no detailed information exists. It can be noted, however, that inflation-
adjusted, per capita police expenditure increased 37 percent between 1970 and
1980 ("Police Employment and Expenditure Trends," *Bureau of Justice Statistics
Special Report*, February 1986). Drug-law enforcement is a subcategory of
"police protection," and these expenditures increased 85 percent at the federal
level, 90 percent at the state level, and 108 percent at the local level over the
period 1976–85 ("Justice Expenditure and Employment, 1985," *Bureau of Justice Statistics Bulletin,* March 1987). Although no statistics are available, drug-
law enforcement as a percentage of total "police protection" has increased over
the period of this study (telephone interview with Ernie O'Boyle, Bureau of
Justice Statistics, September 1987).

the change of relative prices due to risk would predict increases in the average potency of illegal drugs such as marijuana. Information about the potency of marijuana is limited because of the illegal nature of the market, but data have been collected since 1973 by the Potency Monitoring Project sponsored by the National Institute on Drug Abuse (see ElSohly and Abel 1986). The increase in average potency of marijuana from 1974 to 1984 can be clearly seen in figure 6, but the complex nature of this market and severe data limitations preclude a detailed statistical investigation.

To explore the relationship between law enforcement and marijuana potency, I have employed a simple regression using the total drug-law-enforcement budget of selected federal agencies as an explanatory variable for the potency of marijuana. This variable was found to have considerable explanatory power for describing changes in the potency of marijuana (1973–84).[7] The coefficient of the independent variable indicates that an expenditure increase of one million (1972) dollars will result in an increase in potency of .01 of 1 percent. The t statistic of 11.4 indicates that this positive relationship is significant at the .01 level. The R-square statistic indicates that the federal budget devoted to interdiction explains 93 percent of the observed increase in potency ($F = 129.8$). Although problems with simple regression, such as data limitations and specification errors, should of course be recognized, these results indicate that there is more here than just data anomalies.[8] While this test does not

---

[7]No information on potency is available before 1973. The budget for drug-law enforcement increased in 1985–86 (and after), but information is incomplete and is complicated by a large but undisclosed amount of military resources devoted to drug-law enforcement. Potency also continued to increase through 1985–86. The reported average potency did decline as a result of increases in domestic, season-long eradication programs, which greatly increased the percentage of immature and unusable marijuana that was tested for potency. Beginning in 1985–86, most categories of cannabis did increase in potency. These results were originally presented in Thornton 1983 and 1986.

[8]The RESET test was developed by J. Ramsey to detect specification errors. The test was run at the strongest level of significance available. At the .10 level, the F-critical value was 3.07, while the F-statistic was 3.00, indicating no specification error. In order to check further for specification error and time-trend problems, a time-trend variable was added to the original regression. Although the coefficient of this explanatory variable fell, it remained significant at the .05 level ($t = 2.4$).

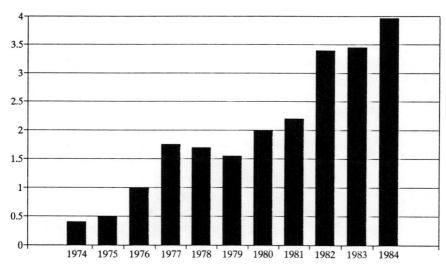

Source: Quarterly Reports of the Marijuana Potency Monitoring Project, National
Institute of Drug Abuse, Oxford, Miss: University of Mississippi, 1974-84.

Note: THC (tetrahydrocannabinol) is the active ingredient in marijuana.

Figure 6. Average Potency of Marijuana, 1973-1984 (percentage THC).

provide unquestionable proof, it does establish "reasonable inferences" about the connection between the enforcement of prohibition, relative prices, and the potency of marijuana.

BEYOND CANNABIS

The potency of many illegal drugs besides marijuana, such as
cocaine, has also increased, and new, highly potent forms of cocaine,
such as "crack," have become available.

Another feature of the modern prohibition of drugs is the substitution of one drug for another. While each drug has some unique
characteristics, most illegal drugs also have some similar attributes.
Changes in relative prices can therefore induce substitution of
lower-priced for higher-priced illegal drugs. For example, Rottenberg (1968, 89n.) argued that individuals were willing to substitute
barbiturates for marijuana on the basis of price.

The recent trend of increased consumption of cocaine may, in
part, be a result of changing relative prices. In 1973 the price of
cocaine was $410 per pure gram, whereas the price of marijuana was

$0.63 per gram (651:1). By 1983 the price of cocaine had fallen to $110 per pure gram, and the price of marijuana had increased to $2.50 per gram (44:1). Even the increased potency of marijuana cannot offset the tremendous decline in the relative price of cocaine (U.S. Department of Justice Bureau of Justice Statistics. 1985, 437).[9]

Another significant aspect of the modern prohibition of drugs is the formulation of new, highly potent products. Both the new products and the increased-potency versions of existing drugs were produced largely with preexisting techniques and technology. Synthetic opiates, for example, can be readily produced using existing techniques. The chemical composition of these extremely powerful drugs can be changed by suppliers to avoid punishment altogether (in the short run) (see Gallagher 1986). It is clear that the availability of extremely potent and dangerous drugs, such as synthetic opiates, is the result of prohibition—not of technological factors.[10] The technology exists to produce the active ingredient in marijuana, THC (tetrahydrocannabinol), in pure form, but the penalties are too low to justify the expense.

The probable cause-and-effect relationship between prohibition and potency is one of the problems that arise with the use of prohibition as a public-policy tool. It may also help to explain the "common wisdom" that marijuana use can lead to heroin addiction. Changes in relative prices in favor of high-potency drugs would lead consumers from marijuana to cocaine and from cocaine to heroin. In the

---

[9]That the absolute price of cocaine would fall in price as enforcement increased may be counterintuitive. The change in absolute prices is a change in relative prices. In 1984 a drug task force dramatically increased its efforts in the Miami area and virtually eliminated the supply of marijuana, but the price of cocaine fell substantially, as marijuana smugglers quickly converted to cocaine smuggling.

[10]In 1967 Arthur D. Little Inc. warned of the potential of these drugs: "If United States law-enforcement policies become so efficient as to prevent altogether the smuggling of heroin, the black market can readily convert to narcotic concentrates that are a thousand or even ten thousand times more potent, milligram for milligram. A few pounds of these concentrates might supply the entire United States addict market for a year. The skills required are not beyond those possessed by the clandestine chemists who now extract morphine from opium and convert the morphine to heroin, or of better chemists who might be recruited" (quoted in Brecher 1972, 96).

extreme, prohibition, law enforcement, and the penalty structure may be more important than the physical properties of drugs in determining what the most dangerous drugs are.

For example, marijuana prohibition is the youngest prohibition, imposes the weakest penalties, and is arguably the least stringently enforced. Methods do exist to increase the average potency of marijuana by five times. In fact, the active ingredient in marijuana, THC, can be produced chemically in nearly pure form, through methods that now appear uneconomical. Nonetheless, these methods could reduce 100 pounds of pre-prohibition marijuana to a sixteen-ounce cola bottle. One would expect that the ingestion of such a quantity to be extremely dangerous, if not fatal. One could further speculate that such a product, produced and consumed in a nonmarket environment, would be nearly as dangerous as heroin. Conversely, heroin prohibition is the oldest of the major prohibitions, involves the most stringent penalties, and is arguably the most strictly enforced given the size of the market.

Compared to their legal predecessors, prohibited products are dramatically lower in quality and higher in potency. The severity of penalties and the intensity of enforcement of the prohibition also determine, in large part, the relative health dangers associated with consuming illegal drugs.[11] Such findings raise fundamental questions about the advisability of employing prohibition of a product to reduce the quantity consumed.

---

[11]Data collected by the Drug Abuse Warning Network established by the National Institute on Drug Abuse indicate that deaths and emergency-room episodes with the higher-potency drugs such as cocaine and heroin have been increasing, but not with other abused drugs.

5

The Corrupting Effects of Prohibition

Heroin abusers are infamous within U.S. society as persons
who criminally victimize others. Involvement in nondrug
criminality among our heroin abusers was indeed common
and even more frequent than has previously been documented.
— (B. D. Johnson et al., *Taking Care of Business:
The Economics of Crime by Heroin Abusers*)

Corruption is a regular effect of interventionism. An analysis
of interventionism would be incomplete if it were not to refer
to the phenomenon of corruption.
— (Ludwig von Mises, *Human Action*)

Several studies have shown an association between the consumption of certain drugs, such as alcohol and heroin, and criminal behavior. This relationship was a crucial reason for the implementation of several prohibitions, including National Alcohol Prohibition, the prohibition of cocaine in several southern states, and the prohibition of marijuana in 1937.

Another motive for enacting prohibition legislation is to reduce corruption of both public officials and the democratic process. People have sold their votes for money or drugs, and the alcohol industry tried to influence elections and public policy. Politicians could also be subject to corruption and blackmail because of alcohol and drugs, and drug use can have a corrupting influence on the actions of political leaders. For these reasons, prohibition was promoted as a means to maintain the integrity of democracy and government.

In general, however, prohibition results in more, not less, crime and corruption. The black markets that result from prohibitions represent institutionalized criminal exchanges. These criminal exchanges, or victimless crimes, often involve violent criminal acts. Prohibitions have also been associated with organized crime and gangs. Violence is used in black markets and criminal organizations to enforce contracts, maintain market share, and defend sales territory.The crime and violence that occurred during the late 1920s and early 1930s was a major reason for the repeal of Prohibition (Kyvig 1979, 123, 167). The nondrug criminal activity of heroin addicts has been associated with the economic effects of prohibition laws and is viewed by Erickson (1969) and others as a major cost of heroin prohibition.

Corruption of law-enforcement officers and other public officials is also a familiar manifestation of prohibited markets. Experience with prohibition has shown it to be a major corrupting influence. The corruption of the Prohibition Bureau proved to be a major stumbling block to the effective enforcement of Prohibition and was also cited as a reason for repeal. Most important, this corruption penetrates beyond the enforcement bureaucracy to government in general. Recent experience has shown that worldwide multidrug prohibition is a major corrupting force in several national governments, such as Colombia and Mexico.

Historical evidence therefore appears to conflict with, or at least to present evidence contrary to, the claims of the prohibitionists. For prohibition to achieve its goals of reducing crime and corruption, several conditions must be met. First, consumption of the product must indeed cause criminal acts and corruption. Second, prohibition must achieve a significant reduction in the consumption of the product without increasing the consumption of other products that cause crime and corruption. Third, prohibition must not lead to significant increases in other forms of crime and corruption.

The use of certain drugs can be considered a contributor to crime. This association along with various other factors may help us describe crime and crime statistics, but they have yet to be established as a sound basis for public policy. First, the use or abuse of certain drugs is not a necessary cause of crime, since crime and corruption can occur without drugs. Second, drugs are also not a sufficient cause of crime because drug use is not by itself able to generate it. Drug use is therefore neither a necessary nor sufficient condition of the criminal activities that prohibition seeks to eliminate or reduce.

If prohibition does reduce certain types of criminal activity while at the same time inducing other criminal activity, then further analysis is required. Several factors, however, argue against reliance on an explicit cost-benefit analysis. First, public policy, I believe, should be based on a generalized approach to prohibition; the specific elasticities examined by cost-benefit analysis are by their very nature unstable and subject to change over time. Second, data on criminal activity are unreliable and in some cases unavailable. Third, the type of criminal activity that prohibition hopes to reduce differs in some cases from the type of criminal behavior induced by prohibition. Fourth, we might expect declines in traditional crime and corruption as prohibition opens up new opportunities and diverts law-enforcement resources.

CRIME

Crime is an important social problem, and a variety of perspectives and theories have been developed to explain its causes. These various approaches can be divided into two categories, economic and environmental, both of which have served as the foundation for public policy.

The general understanding of human action provided by the market-process method is particularly valuable for developing an evaluation of these approaches. It also provides a framework in which the empirical investigations and policy pronouncements can be evaluated and incorporated. Prohibition provides a valuable case study for improving our understanding of crime and social control.

Two Views of Crime

Early notions concerning the causes of crime were firmly grounded on economic factors. Thomas More, Beccaria-Bonesana, Adam Smith, and Frederick Engels all found crime to be associated with poverty and economic conditions. The utilitarian philosopher-economist Jeremy Bentham (1896) argued that criminal behavior was entirely rational. Bentham's pleasure-versus-pain analysis implicitly incorporates both the low opportunity cost of crime to the poor with the relatively high-value opportunities provided by crime. W. A. Bonger (1916) found that the work of several early French statisticians supported the relationship between crime and economic conditions.

Although crime was viewed as individualistic and economic in nature, all these early commentators called for solutions which were primarily governmental in nature. Even Adam Smith ([1776] 1976) argued for governmental intervention in the area of crime, deeming it one of the three fundamental duties of government, although he had argued the opposite earlier.

Nothing tends so much to corrupt mankind as dependency, while independency still increases the honesty of the people. The establishment of commerce and manufactures, which brings about this independency, is the best policy for preventing crimes. The common people have better wages in this way than in any other, and in consequence of this a general probity of manners takes place through the whole country. Nobody will be so mad as to expose himself upon the highway, when he can make better bread in an honest and industrious manner. (Smith [1763] 1956, 155–56)

Smith's remarks in 1776 apparently held more sway with English authorities. Experiments in the use of a police force began in 1786 in Ireland and, in a less ruthless form, in England beginning with the Metropolitan Police Act of 1829. As Stanley H. Palmer (1988) has shown, many of the national police forces were formed to deal with those opposed to the government, rather than to fight common crime.

A second theory of criminal behavior emphasizes environmental and genetic factors, disputes the relevance of the economic theory of crime, and claims that criminal behavior is related to characteristics such as the configuration of the skull, reflex activity, race, age, sex, and social class. This sociological paradigm began to displace the early economic approach around the turn of the nineteenth century. For example, Cesare Lombroso argued that criminals were a subspecies of man possessing special characteristics such as unique facial structure or unusually long arms (described in Pyle 1983, 5).

The association of drug use with crime would be classified with the sociological approach to criminal behavior because it is based on observation and probability rather than theory. This sociological theory differs from earlier versions in that it attributes the cause of crime primarily to environmental factors, rather than to genetic ones.

Timberlake (1963, 56–61) noted that progressive sociologists and criminologists who espoused this view opposed liquor use because of its association with a large number of criminal acts and undesirable behavior. For example, in a study of prison inmates, John Koren (1899) concluded that alcohol was the sole cause of 16 percent of all crimes, the primary cause of 31 percent, and a contributing cause of 50 percent. This theory was a two-edged sword, however; it helped establish prohibitions, but it removed cause and guilt from criminal acts. Prisoners began to exaggerate the role that alcohol played in their commission of crimes and to ignore the more serious causes (Timberlake 1963, 58). During the early years of marijuana prohibition, some convicts petitioned for leniency on the basis of their use of marijuana, which, they said, had caused their crimes rather than they themselves.

The Marxist perspective on crime has been a traditional justification for Marxist theory. As a branch of the environmental approach, it contains an element of the economic approach, viewing crime as a reaction of the proletariat to economic development. Rather than genetics, physical features, or drug use, social class is the factor that identifies potential criminals.

Contrary to the early Adam Smith ([1763] 1956), economic development is viewed as the cause of crime rather than a cure. Marxists point to increased crime rates in "capitalist" countries and urban areas as evidence of the viability of the overall Marxist philosophy and beliefs.

The Economics of Crime

According to Paul H. Rubin (1978, 38), "Until about 1968 most academic research on crime was done by sociologists. The basic premise of this work seems to have been that criminals were somehow different from noncriminals, and the major research consisted of searching for the ways in which criminals differed." Gary S. Becker (1968) reestablished the study of crime and punishment as rational and economic. His contribution has been challenged, refined, tested, and extended. This body of research has come to dominate the modern approach to crime and has had some visible effects on public policy. For example, Isaac Ehrlich's publications

(1973, 1975) based on Becker were cited by the Supreme Court in reestablishing the death penalty. Three law professors who helped extend Becker's economic approach to crime (Robert Bork, Richard Posner, and Antonin Scalia) received high judicial appointments.

Becker's (1968) time-allocation model of criminal behavior is formulated in terms of the subjective expected utility of the individual. The individual is shown to form subjective expectations about the probability of arrest and the severity and likelihood of punishment. The potential criminal weighs the subjective value of the expected gain from crime against these costs. The results derived from this model imply that increases in the probability of capture and severity of punishment will deter crime.

The explicit modeling of crime in economic terms presents some problems. For example, it is difficult to speak of a market supply of crime, and even more difficult to speak of a market demand for crime. Markets of crime rarely if ever exist, and crimes such as rape, robbery, and murder simply cannot be called voluntary transactions. These models convert the benefits of crime into purely monetary terms, despite the fact that the benefits of crimes of passion and violence are primarily nonmonetary and extremely difficult to translate into monetary terms.

These models are based on subjectively determined evaluations, but in econometric "testing," objective or actual measures of the probability of capture and expected punishment are employed. These deviations from theory that are necessary to obtain empirical verification of theory tend to cloak important nuances of criminal behavior, punishment, police behavior, and the criminal firm, thereby limiting our understanding of crime. Samuel Cameron (1989) and others have found, for example, that the puzzling correlations between crime, arrest rates, and police resources "are to be explained in large part by the failure of economists to measure the criminal's subjective expectations in the subjective expected–utility model" (36).

The Economics of Prohibition Crime

Prohibition creates new profit opportunities for both criminals and noncriminals. For people already engaged in criminal careers, prohibitions provide new and enhanced profit opportunities that may increase the number of crimes they commit or alter the type of crimes they commit. Robbers may become bootleggers, or loansharks may expand into drug dealing. For example, Al Capone expanded his business from gambling and prostitution to bootlegging during Prohibition. The new and expanded profit opportunities will also bring new players into criminal pursuits; these new entrants are likely to come from the consumers of the prohibited product.

The enforcement of prohibition results in higher prices for illegal products, which in turn has a detrimental effect on the consumers of the prohibited product. Some consumers will respond to higher prices by reducing or eliminating their consumption of the product in question—others will not. Consumers who have formed habits, or addictions, to a particular good will remain in the market. They could be classified as having an inelastic demand for the prohibited good in the relevant price range. These consumers will therefore consume less of all other goods (food, clothing, shelter, medical care) as a consequence of prohibition.

For example, a heroin consumer responds to a 1000 percent increase in price by reducing consumption by 50 percent (figure 7). This inelastic response entails a reduction in the consumption of all other goods, shown by a shift in the budget line in figure 8.

The consumer's initial budget constraint in figure 8 was predetermined by the choice between labor and leisure. The labor-leisure trade-off, however, is also affected by prohibition in a nonconventional way. The tremendous increase in the price of heroin during prohibition results in a new budget constraint. For the individual who has a highly inelastic demand for heroin, prohibition is akin to a famine which increases food prices several hundred percent. The increased price of prohibited products will have little or no effect on nominal wage rates, so real wage rates (purchasing power) fall. Falling real wage rates normally increases leisure time (little consolation for heroin addicts), but here we might expect more labor time or a switch to a job that pays higher wage rates in order to compensate for greater risks (for example, crime). In any case, the heroin user is much worse off and under stress.

In figure 9, income from legal and illegal activity is measured against the amount of risk from criminal activities undertaken by heroin users. Legal income (in terms of purchasing power) is measured along the vertical axis. Illegal income is measured as an expected income line from the vertical axis. Expected income from

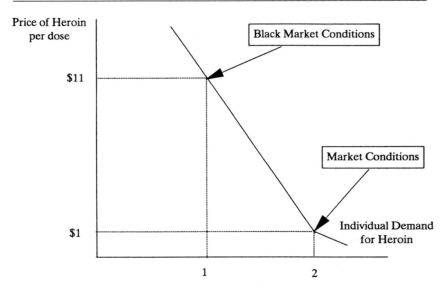

Figure 7. The Impact of Prohibition on the Consumption of Heroin.

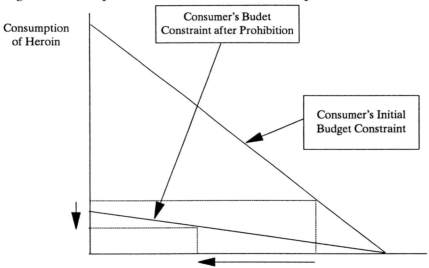

Figure 8. Prohibition's Impact on the Heroin Addict's Budget Constraint.

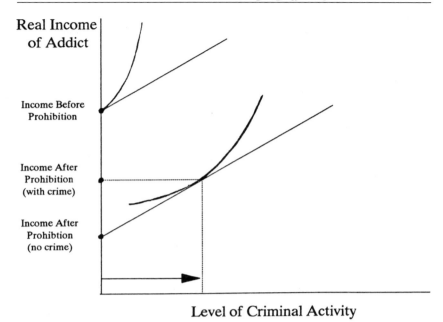

Figure 9. Prohibition's Impact on (addict-related) Criminal Activity.

crime is assumed to increase with the level of criminal activity. Reuter et al. (1990) have completed a study of drug dealers in Washington D.C., which indicates that dealers trade risk for money. They find dealing drugs on the streets presents high risks, while the "profits" are modest.

Indifference curves that indicate crime (risk) as bad have been superimposed on the graph. In the absence of prohibition, consumers with high incomes will be more risk-averse to crime due to the threat of losing their freedom, income, future income, reputation, and so on. Prohibition's depressing effect on the real wage rates of heroin consumers will induce them to become criminals as their opportunity cost of illegal activities declines.

At the initial income level the individual will engage in little or no illegal activity. As the price of heroin increases, real income falls. At this lower level of income the relative rewards of illegal income are enhanced. The individual will increase their level of criminal activity. Therefore, prohibition will induce some noncriminals into illegal activities such as drug dealing or robbery.

The supply of criminal activity from noncriminal drug users can be viewed as function of the severity of prohibition enforcement. The level of prohibition enforcement is positively related to the price of the prohibited product, and therefore it is negatively related to the real income of addicts and habitual users. The decreased real income from prohibition makes illegal income more attractive. Therefore the higher price for heroin results in more criminal activity. George F. Brown and Lester P. Silverman 1974 presented evidence of this relationship in the short run. Changes in the level of enforcement may also affect the type of criminal activity. For example, as more resources are devoted to prohibition enforcement, property crimes such as burglary become less risky and therefore increase in number. Benson et al. (1990) have shown that increased efforts to suppress illegal drugs have resulted in decreased enforcement efforts against property crime and thus an increase in it.

The Historical Trend in Crime

Theoretically, prohibition increases crime from both the "supply" and "demand" side. Statistically, we would also expect crime to increase because of prohibition "crimes" and the incidental crimes of the underground economy such as those connected with defining market territories and enforcing contracts. Empirical investigations of the causes of crime and changes in crime rates have been notoriously difficult and inaccurate. An overview of the historical trend in crime provides an opportunity to evaluate various theories of crime and the neglected relationship between it and prohibition. According to the economic (market-process) approach to crime, economic development will result in less criminal activity and prohibition will result in greater amounts of crime (in addition to violations of prohibition law). The expected increase in crime due to prohibition is a function of the degree of both enforcement and the underlying demand for the prohibited product.

The Marxist theory of crime has been a major focus of the study of criminal behavior. This theory holds that economic development results in an increasing gap between the rich and the poor and an increasing rate of "crises." Workers respond to exploitation, alienation, urbanization, and crisis by committing more crimes against capitalism and the upper classes. In support of their theory, Marxists point to the increasing crime during the nineteenth century and recent times in capitalist countries. Lynn McDonald (1976) showed that consensus, biological, and conflict theorists all agree that crime is related to economic development (for different reasons) and that crime rates rose during the nineteenth century.

The nineteenth century was indeed a period of fruition for capitalism, but it was not a pure market economy. In banking, transportation, and education, the seeds were sown for tremendous increases in government interventionism. Also, several points must be raised concerning the evidence on crime that supposedly supports Marxism. First, the urbanization and economic development that occurred between the 1830s and the twentieth century were accompanied by decreased rates of severe and violent crimes. Second, increases in crime rates were largely due to increases in minor crimes, such as public drunkenness. Urban societies apparently become less tolerant of mischievous behavior as population concentrations increase and economic activity becomes more organized. Third, police forces were established in major urban areas during the middle of the nineteenth century. This unquestionably led to an increase in both the awareness of criminal activity and the collection of statistics on crime (Lane 1968). Fourth, and most important, crime rates have been found to have declined, rather than increased, during the nineteenth century in the major capitalist countries, including the United States (McDonald 1982). These latter two points suggest that, contrary to the Marxian explanation, capitalist development results in decreased crime and more social-control mechanisms.

An early example of the impact of prohibition on crime (and a deviation from capitalism) was the liquor control legislation in Massachusetts from 1838 to 1840. While this prohibition actually established the requirement of a fifteen-gallon minimum purchase and was only in effect for two years, several instructive lessons endure. The fifteen-gallon minimum can be viewed as an attempt to use the political process to achieve immediately the social control that only slowly and methodically develops under capitalism. This impatience with capitalism does, however, reflect the general decreased tolerance of disruptive public behavior mentioned earlier.

If prohibition was an outgrowth of intolerance, its intended effect—in the short run—was not achieved. In this more rowdy era, antitemperance forces countered what they considered aggression against their rights (for example, temperance legislation) with aggression. Robert L. Hampel (1982, 90) notes that the severity of criminal activity was correlated with the severity of temperance legislation. "Before and after the experiment with prohibition, vandalism and ridicule were the principal means of harassment. Shaving horse tails, girdling trees, or defacing the front of houses were standard from anti-temperance rowdies. But with the passage of the 15 Gallon Law, physical assaults and mob demonstrations became more common. Where an 1834 Taunton incident involved the tarring and feathering of several homes, the same criminals in 1839 might have gone after the homeowners instead."

The fifteen-gallon law was both difficult and costly to enforce. The total number of crimes, especially alcohol-license violations, increased significantly. The increased number of violations in turn caused delays in the court and a rapid decline in the conviction rate on all crimes (Hampel 1982, 99–100). This short episode with prohibition resulted in more crime, more violent crime, delay in the courts, and a lower conviction rate on all crimes.

Contrary to Marxist views and early impressions, crime has decreased during economic progress. Eric H. Monkkonen (1981) has reviewed the studies of crime during the nineteenth and early twentieth centuries and has found that only two studies (using individual city data) contradict the trend toward decreased crime. It is only during the Prohibition era that anomalies in national criminal statistics start to occur. For example, Monkkonen (1981, 555) notes that the percentage of crimes that were appealed decreased from before 1870 to 1939, except during the decade of the 1920s. It can be reasonably assumed that the rate of serious crimes was declining because appeals generally represent crimes of a serious nature.

Some observers have suggested that the "crime wave" during Prohibition was just a mere impression, a fabrication of media hype. Even a leading wet, Dr. Fabian Franklin, stated that the "crime wave is a state of mind" (quoted in Fisher 1928, 76). Observers such as Franklin, however, fail to address the nature of changes in the composition of crime, the long-run decline in crime rates before Prohibition, and the social upheaval beginning with World War I.

For example, Franklin notes that crime declined by 37.7 percent during the period 1910–23. This is, however, attributable to a decline in less serious crime—crimes involving violence or theft of property increased by 13.2 percent. Homicide increased 16.1 percent and robbery rose by 83.3 percent over the period, while crime such as vagrancy and malicious mischief decreased by over 50 percent (Fisher 1928, 77). While dismissing the significance of alcohol and drug-prohibition crimes, Franklin does note that the increased homicide rate may be related to "the illegal traffic" (quoted in Fisher 1928, 80).

Fisher himself hints that changes in criminal statistics may have resulted from the new profitable opportunities created by Prohibition and the Harrison Narcotics Act. Fisher's "interesting suggestion" is essentially to interpret criminal statistics of the Prohibition era using the economic, or market-process, perspective. First, serious crime had been on the decline over a long period of economic development (approximately 1800–1910), while less serious crime was increasing. Higher standards of living, increased expectations of living standards, and increased urbanization had made people less tolerant of unseemly public behavior. The growth in minor crime was thus partly the result of a greater number of unlawful offenses. The subsequent decrease in petty crime and increase in serious crime can therefore be explained by the impact of prohibitions on criminal opportunities.

Warburton (1932) provides evidence which indicates that homicide rates (in large cities) increased significantly from 1910 to 1933; this period includes the third wave of state prohibitions (1910–19), the Harrison Narcotics Act (1914), wartime restrictions on alcohol (1918–19), and Prohibition (1920–33). The greater number of federal prisoners provides further evidence of more serious crime during Prohibition. The number of prisoners in federal prisons, reformatories, and camps grew from 3,889 in 1920 to 13,698 in 1932 (Wooddy 1934, 90–99).

The increase in crime during the 1920s has been described without reference to Prohibition. For example, John A. Pandiani (1982) noted: "A major wave of crime appears to have begun as early as the mid 1920's [and] increased continually until 1933 . . . when it mysteriously reversed itself" (349). The sudden change in the direction of crime rates was mysterious to many observers because they were predisposed to the Marxian and business–cycle approach to crime. The description of crime statistics put forth by Theodore A. Ferdinand (1967) also recounts a dramatic and "mysterious" decline beginning in 1933 that lasted throughout the 1930s.

Andrew F. Henry and James F. Short (1954) attempted to show that the increased crime from 1929 to 1933 was the result of variations in business activity. Philip J. Cook and Gary A. Zarkin (1985), however, have found that the "major movements in crime rates during the last half century cannot be attributed to the business cycle" (128). Pandiani (1982) attempted to account for the decrease in crime starting in 1933 by showing that the Civilian Conservation Corps (CCC) removed many potential criminals from society.

Fluctuation in economic activity and major government programs such as the CCC no doubt played some role in these criminal statistics, but Prohibition appears to be the significant explanatory variable for changes in the crime rate and the composition of crime. The repeal of Prohibition appears to be the best explanation for the dramatic reversal in 1933 and the return to the long-run decline in crime rates. The two alternative theories have a difficult time explaining the continuous decrease in crime during the remainder of the 1930s.

The resumption of the decline in criminal activity after 1933 is not the result of the absence of all prohibition, but rather the repeal of the most significant prohibition—alcohol. The Harrison Narcotics Act still applied, and marijuana was prohibited in 1937. The use of narcotics and marijuana, however, was insignificant compared with the consumption of alcohol. Budgets for the enforcement of narcotics and marijuana prohibitions were curtailed and enforcement was lax. In addition, after the repeal of Prohibition, the falling price of alcohol provided a low-priced substitute for illegal substances.

According to the theory that crime is based on its association with intoxicants such as alcohol, easy access to alcohol after repeal should have led to increased crime. As Cook and Zarkin (1985, 117) note, "intoxication has long been thought to be an important cause of crime, particularly violent crime." The evidence they present, however, suggests that the rates for murder, burglary, robbery, and auto theft declined after the repeal of Prohibition, resuming the long secular decline. The national homicide rate declined from the last year of Prohibition to the early 1960s. Eric H. Monkkonen (1981, 556–57) notes that the return to increasing consumption per capita after repeal is associated with fewer arrests for drunk and disorderly conduct. In any case, the consumption of alcohol appears to be a poor explanatory variable; often it is negatively related to crime rates.

Crime rates again deviated from long-run trends in the mid-1960s, when prohibition once again became a significant public policy. Increased exposure of servicemen to drugs during the Vietnam War, resistance to the war, demographic factors increased the demand for drugs such as marijuana. Increased efforts to suppress these markets began what has become known as the war on drugs.

James Q. Wilson and Richard J. Herrnstein (1985, 409) note that the homicide rate began increasing in the mid-1960s and then increased at an alarming rate. According to national crime statistics, the number of murders, burglaries, robberies, and auto thefts, which had been decreasing, began to increase during the 1960s. The rise in crime became dramatic during the late 1960s, leading the Nixon administration to begin its crackdown on drugs. Crime rates continued to increase throughout the 1970s and 1980s.

Prohibition is not the only explanation for the increase in crime over the last quarter century. For example, the philosophy of the justice system has undergone a change from the punishment, restitution, and isolation of criminals to their rehabilitation and reintegration into society. The state, therefore, now acts as a surrogate victim in the absence of a true victim. and the criminal has become a victim of society. The increased use of plea bargaining, probation, commuted sentences, release on bail, community-based correction programs, and the insanity and diminished-capacity defense have made crime easier and have been justified in part by the overcrowding of prisons (see Bidinotto 1989).

Black markets become more organized over time just as legal markets do. Two manifestations of the greater degree of organization are crime syndicates and street gangs. Organized crime has long been associated with prohibition. Prohibitions against prostitution, gambling, "high" interest rates, and the consumption of drugs have served as the basis for virtually all known crime syndicates. Humbert S. Nelli (1985) shows that syndicates that developed during Prohibition survived long after repeal. Street gangs profit and expand based on their role in organizing retail drug sales. Their violent criminal activity has been a growing and very visible result of the war on drugs during the 1980s and 1990s. Gangs also developed in the late 1920s in response to the profit potential provided by Prohibition. In 1930 Frederick Thrasher, a sociologist, warned of the growing threat of gangs. He noted that the economic incentive led gangs to work for criminals and racketeers (Pandiani 1982, 349).

As predicted by Adam Smith, capitalistic economic development tends to reduce the rate of crime. As economic development and its concomitants (for example, urbanization) proceed, new rules, guidelines, and controls on antisocial public behavior are established to deal with the greater complexities of economic life. Deviations from capitalism, such as prohibition, have disrupted the long-term trends toward decreased crime. Crime was shown to increase and become more violent during the time of the fifteen–gallon law in Massachusetts, during Prohibition, and since the late 1960s when enforcement of the prohibition on narcotics and marijuana began to be more rigorous. Further, crime was shown to decrease during nonprohibition periods, although consumption of intoxicants was increasing per capita.

In addition, the theory that prohibition causes crime has been confirmed by the observations of Johnson and his colleagues (1985). They found explicit empirical evidence that narcotics prohibition could be directly related to crimes other than illegal drug sale and use. Sociologists, however, have tended to isolate prohibition from the general study of crime and have failed, along with criminologists and economists, to consider prohibition a worthwhile variable in the explanation of crime rates. While prohibition is certainly not the only cause of crime, its inclusion would improve both the empirical study of theories of crime and the study of the trends in crime rates. The empirical evidence examined in this section indicates that prohibition has increased crime and has imposed a significant cost on society.

CORRUPTION

The control of corruption is of vital interest in any free and democratic society. An important goal of prohibition is the reduction of corruption. Timberlake (1963) claims that political corruption by the alcohol industry was the major reason for establishing Prohibition: "Like many other businesses, the liquor industry sought to influence or control all levels of government in order to promote its interests and to protect itself against unfavorable legislation. But unlike most businesses, it had a special reason to engage in politics: no other enterprise paid such high taxes or contributed such large sums to government" (106). Prohibition seeks to reduce corruption in both the specific sense of the bribery of public officials and in the general sense of maintaining individual integrity, virtue, and moral principles. Experience, however, shows that, on the contrary, the corruption of public officials increases. As Mises notes, "Unfortunately the office-holders and their staffs are not angelic. They learn very soon that their decisions mean for the businessmen either considerable losses or—sometimes—considerable gains. Certainly there are also bureaucrats who do not take bribes; but there are others who are anxious to take advantage of any 'safe' opportunity of 'sharing with those whom their decisions favor' " (1949, 734). This corruption, in the case of prohibition, represents a failure to achieve the goals of prohibition and a major impediment to the enforcement of prohibition.

Academic interest in the corruption of public officials has been growing and appears to be related to the amount of corruption that occurs. The first flurry of research on corruption occurred during the latter half of Prohibition and in the aftermath of repeal. The rate of publication began to increase substantially in the 1960s and apparently peaked in 1975 (Simpson 1977 and Duchaine 1979). The rate of publication remained high throughout the rest of the 1970s, although it seems to have declined somewhat in the 1980s.

The amount of corruption detected has been increasing in recent years. Federal convictions of corrupt public officials has increased from 44 in 1970 to 1067 in 1988 (figure 10). The substantial jump in indictments and convictions in 1983 has been explained by an increased focus on corruption and better reporting of lower-level corruption. While corruption due to prohibition occurs in all areas of government, the federal efforts seem to have been most successful in convicting state and local enforcement officials. Based on the representative cases, 75 percent of state and local law-enforcement corruption is directly related to prohibition (U.S. Department of Justice 1989, 30).

The Economics of Corruption

The literature on corruption generally agrees that corruption is rational, systemic, and functional. The individual participants in cor-

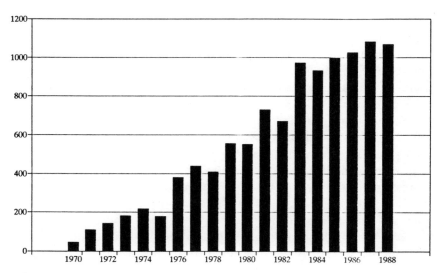

Source: U.S. Department of Justice, Criminal Division, "Report to Congress on the Activities and Operations of the Public Integrity Section for 1981," p. 20; "1988," p. 29, U.S. Department of Justice, Washington, DC. (mimeographed.)

Figure 10. Federal Convictions of Public Officials: 1970-1988.

ruption are viewed as pursuing their self-interest at the expense of the general, or public, interest. Corruption has also been found to be a characteristic feature of government, particularly of the law–enforcement function. The "function" of corruption is to facilitate transactions when control over transactions has been delegated to government.

Many general definitions of corruption have been put forward. In the legal world corruption is a failure in the principal-agent relationship. The economics of the legal approach is best illustrated in the work of Banfield (1975). This definition is open-ended and applies to both government and the market. In another definition corruption occurs anytime an agent of the government acts to promote self-interest over the public interest. Modern economists, on the other hand, view all action as self-interested, and thus this definition is inappropriate. Interest-group legislation is self-interested, but economists view it as rent seeking, not corruption.

Economists such as Murray N. Rothbard (1970), Susan Rose-Ackerman (1975), and Bruce L. Benson (1981) have defined corrup-

tion as the illegal sale or purchase of property rights. In this definition corruption is rational, systemic, and functional. It is legalistic,
but not universal in scope. For example, it once was legal to sell one's
vote, but it no longer is. Therefore, vote buying is now viewed as a
corrupt practice. It is illegal for law-enforcement agents to accept
tips and compensation directly from the people they serve in the
United States, but it is both legal and acceptable in other societies.
The lack of universality does not affect the analysis of corruption; in
fact, it facilitates recommendations for reform.

While most disciplines have sought to discover the function of
corruption, economists have searched for the source or cause of corruption. Rothbard (1970) views corruption as a consequence of government intervention. Activities in the market that are similar to
corruption are either transactions or crimes, such as theft. Far from
dismissing the possibility of private individual involvement in corruption, however, this perspective suggests that private citizens do
become corrupt, but only as a consequence of government intervention. Even the opponents of the view that corruption is solely the
result of government intervention, such as Rose-Ackerman (1978),
fail to provide an example of corruption in a purely competitive
market.

Corruption is therefore a cost of government intervention. Most
modern research on corruption and its control seeks as its objective
the optimization or minimization, rather than the elimination, of
corruption. Bruce L. Benson and John Baden (1985, 393) claim that
"it is impossible to drive the level of government corruption to
zero." If all the costs of government intervention, however, including
corruption and its control, are considered (and Benson and Baden
make a point of this [410]), it is conceivable that zero corruption
could be achieved by eliminating all government (or nearly so) or by
eliminating the tax-based foundation and property-rights-determi-
nation functions of government.

Corruption occurs at all levels of government, and it involves
politicians, bureaucrats, law-enforcement officials, and private individuals. Corruption can be associated with four areas of government
activity: government procurement, public finance (taxation), election fraud, and regulation. In the first three categories, corruption is
a function of the size of government. Prohibition, along with price
controls and building codes, would come under the heading of regu-

lation. This type of corruption is related to the stringency of regulation on property rights and the resulting profit opportunities. Therefore, to understand corruption resulting from prohibition, an analysis of property rights and their value must be undertaken.

The economics of corruption is best developed in the work of Benson (1981, 1988) and Benson and Baden (1985), in which corruption is seen as the result of government control over property rights. Political corruption essentially is the illegal sale of property rights by those in government to private individuals. The incentives for corruption are adapted from Becker's (1968) analysis of crime. Corruption depends on its expected payoff, the probability of detection, and the severity of punishment. The extent of corruption is shown to be an increasing function of the size of government (408–10).

Benson (1988) applied the property-rights approach to the corruption of criminal justice officials. He found the criminal justice system to be a major source of corruption. He also found that corruption accelerates if law-enforcement budgets, the number of crimes, and police discretion continue to increase. Not only are the number of officials who can allocate property rights increasing, the incentive to sell these rights is increasing. Detection is also less likely as the criminal justice system expands while resources to monitor the system are "relatively fixed" (157–59).

Corruption and Prohibition

In addition to these contributions to the economics of corruption, several contributors to the economics of heroin prohibition, such as Rottenberg (1968) and Moore (1977), have described in detail the role and effects of corruption in prohibition enforcement, the costs and benefits to the corrupting parties, and methods of reducing corruption.

Drug prohibition represents a fundamental change in property rights, which are subject to the forces of rent seeking and corruption. By far the most important and direct source of corruption, however, is the black-market activity resulting from prohibition. Prohibition creates illicit profit opportunities that would not exist in its absence. The enforcement of prohibition creates profit opportunities for the agents of the government who are best able and most willing to take advantage of them. These profit opportunities result in corruption of public officials.

Two results of the enforcement of prohibition play an instrumental role in the corruption of public officials. The higher price caused by increased enforcement enables suppliers to cover the costs of risk bearing and avoiding detection. Suppliers can lessen some of the risk by agreement with public officials. This reduction results from the public official's failure to enforce the prohibition law against a supplier (the briber), his participation in the shipment of prohibited products, or his selective enforcement of prohibition against competitors of the briber. In return for this protection, the public official receives money, quantities of the illegal products, or if blackmail is involved, the silence of the briber.

Corruption is a function of the price of the prohibited product. As enforcement increases, the price of a prohibited product and the costs of avoiding detection rise relative to the basic costs of production. We should expect that suppliers would be willing to pay to reduce their risk. A higher price involves both a greater risk of apprehension and a greater incentive to provide monetary payments to public officials.

As enforcement increases, the risk of apprehension rises and the quantity of output decreases. The divergence between price and the basic costs of production increases. Increased enforcement therefore increases the ratio of costs of risk to the cost of production. The result is an increased profit opportunity for entrepreneurship in avoiding detection. Many avenues exist by which entrepreneurs can reduce detection risks. They can use faster boats and planes, smaller and easier-to-conceal products, or deceptive packaging. One way to shift the burden of risk is to corrupt the public officials charged with the enforcement of prohibition. As enforcement efforts increase, corruption (like potency) will gain a comparative advantage in avoiding detection over transportation, technology, and deception. We therefore expect corruption to increase with increased enforcement efforts, whether or not total revenues in the industry increase. This assumes that the underlying demand for the product, penalties for both prohibition and corruption, and the efforts to reduce corruption are held constant.

Suppliers in black markets pay public officials to provide protection or risk reduction to them. Public officials are able to reduce the risk to suppliers, but they also face the risk of losing a prestigious and high-paying job. This higher cost to public officials is offset by a higher payoff from the suppliers, based on the value of illegal transactions. The value of drug transactions within the jurisdiction of a public official is typically hundreds of times larger than the official's annual salary.

The literature on crime suggests that the commission of one crime can have a tremendous effect on the subjective evaluation of the costs of committing additional crimes. The cost of the first criminal act is high due to uncertainty and lack of familiarity with crime. When an official commits one act of corruption, the costs of additional acts decline, in a fashion similar to the marginal cost of production in a firm.

One important factor in the entry of public officials into corruption is their familiarity with rent seeking. Public-choice theory views the public official as being in the business of selling property rights to interest groups. Rent-seeking behavior is "corruption" in the broader sense. This exposure to "corruption" would seem to make politicians particularly vulnerable to the more narrowly conceived corruption.

The incentives of both suppliers and government officials combine to form mutual profit opportunities. Moore (1977) and Rose-Ackerman (1978) provide a description of the actual forms of corruption and the constraints faced by suppliers and public officials.

Increased enforcement also has an interactive effect on drug potency and bribery, since it changes capital requirements. More physical capital is required in order to increase the potency of existing drugs or to produce higher-potency drugs. Higher potency generally requires more refining and more complex capital equipment. Fixed capital, however, is susceptible to detection in an already risky environment. Again, bribery becomes a cost-effective technique for reducing risk compared with other methods, such as concealment.

In addition to capital requirements, corruption accelerates for the reasons described by Benson and Baden (1985). In their analysis, growth in government increases the difficulty of monitoring and controlling employees. A diminished rate of detection combined with greater payoffs will accelerate corruption.

Corruption during Prohibition

The history of corruption in America dates back to the founding of the country. The literature on the history of corruption represents a variety of perspectives. Three major trends can be garnered from an examination of this literature. First, whether corruption is viewed as a "people" problem or as an institutional problem, it is both persistent and positively related to government control of society. Second, while persistent and "petty" corruption cannot be eliminated in government, it can be minimized through the use of controls and higher salaries for enforcement officials, as noted in Becker and Stigler (1974). Third, corruption is a pervasive factor in governments that attempt to enforce victimless crime laws. Because of the lack of a self-interested injured party, corruption due to prohibition is more difficult to detect than corruption associated with government contracts, minimum wage laws, or rent controls.

Corruption was a major feature of Prohibition and many researchers have found a causal connection between the two. Gerald Astor (1971) noted the connection between police corruption in New York City and Prohibition during the 1920s. Emanuel H. Lavine (1936) provides a journalistic account of it. Edward D. Sullivan ([1929] 1971) found that a large segment of the criminal population consisted of law-enforcement officials and that the major corrupting influences were gambling and Prohibition. Mark H. Haller (1970), investigating corruption in Chicago in the early twentieth century, found that reformers who wanted control of prostitution, gambling, and alcohol were ineffective because they attacked police corruption. In contrast, businessmen achieved protection from property crimes, which generally did not lead to police corruption. Lear B. Reed (1941) showed that the nature of crime and corruption in Kansas City was different before and after Prohibition and recommended that politics be divorced from law-enforcement policy. Reginald W. Kauffman (1923) also concluded that the corruption found during Prohibition was inherent in bootlegging and was further stimulated by the political nature of law-enforcement officials. A. F. Brandstatter (1962) found that a general disrespect for the law resulted from the corruption that occurred under the Volstead Act.

The Wickersham Report (1931) provides a review of the first ten years of Prohibition. The emphasis on corruption points to the fact that it played an important role in Prohibition. It should be noted that the original organization of Prohibition law enforcement was not satisfactory. Reorganization in 1927 placed employees under Civil Service requirements. By June 1930 more than 1,600 employees had been dismissed for causes often related to corruption or dereliction of duty. Detection of corruption and resulting dismissals did decrease in 1929 and 1930, "yet to the extent that these conditions have existed or may now exist, they constitute important factors in the problem of prohibition enforcement and are vital considerations as affecting the government generally" (Wickersham Report 1931, 17). As the report goes on to note, the number of dismissals represents only a fraction of the actual wrongdoing by enforcement officials and does not include wrongdoing by others outside the Prohibition unit. Civil Service reform, rather than reducing the amount of actual wrongdoing, may really reduce reporting of wrongdoing in order to maintain the reputation of bureaucracies in the interest of lifelong bureaucrats.

In evaluating the negative aspects of Prohibition the report begins:

As to corruption it is sufficient to refer to the reported decisions of the courts during the past decade in all parts of the country, which reveal a succession of prosecutions for conspiracies, sometimes involving the police, prosecuting and administrative organizations of whole communities; to the flagrant corruption disclosed in connection with diversions of industrial alcohol and unlawful production of beer; to the record of federal prohibition administration as to which cases of corruption have been continuous and corruption has appeared in services which in the past had been above suspicion; to the records of state police organizations; to the revelations as to police corruption in every type of municipality, large and small, throughout the decade; to the conditions as to prosecution revealed in surveys of criminal justice in many parts of the land; to the evidence of connection between corrupt local politics and gangs and the organized unlawful liquor traffic, and of systematic collection of tribute from that traffic, for corrupt political purposes. There have been other eras of corruption. . . . But the present regime of corruption in connection with the liquor traffic is operating in a new and larger field and is more extensive. (Wickersham Report 1931, 44)

Herbert Hoover had organized the National Commission on Law Observance and Enforcement (known as the Wickersham Commission from the name of its head, George W. Wickersham) to improve on the enforcement of Prohibition. Instead he received a report that questioned the effectiveness of Prohibition and in which many dissenting opinions were voiced. In the separate statements by members of the commission, almost all voiced opposition to Prohibition.

The strongest statement against Prohibition was made by Harry Anderson, who noted the existence of pervasive corruption and argued that the problems of Prohibition would not improve with reorganization because they were systemic and might cause problems beyond the confines of the drink problem. He noted: "These principles of economic law are fundamental. They cannot be resisted or ignored. Against their ultimate operation the mandates of laws and constitutions and the powers of government appear to be no more effective than the broom of King Canute against the tides of the sea" (Wickersham Report 1931, 97). Anderson also admitted that effective enforcement was a possibility, but only at an expenditure beyond all practical limitations. He noted that even with complete enforcement, economic laws would prevail: "This would inevitably lead to social and political consequences more disastrous than the evils sought to be remedied. Even then the force of social and economic laws would ultimately prevail. These laws cannot be destroyed by governments, but often in the course of human history governments have been destroyed by them" (98). While many of the members of the commission agreed with Anderson on most points, enough of them wanted further experimentation with Prohibition that the commission's final recommendations were diluted.

The prohibition of narcotics, gambling, and prostitution has also been shown to cause a great deal of corruption. Ralph L. Smith (1965), Leonard Shecter and William R. Phillips (1973), Robert H. Williams (1973), and James Mills (1986) all show the prevalence of corruption due to these prohibitions. Corruption associated with narcotics has largely been associated with the biggest single market for heroin and other narcotics, New York City. The Knapp Commission on Police Corruption in New York City found "significant levels of corruption" within the Narcotics Division of the New York City Police Department and at other levels of government (Moore 1977, 193–95). Richard Kunnes (1972) provides some anecdotal evidence for the argument above as it relates to the prohibition of heroin: "Profits are so great that corruption of law enforcement officials has become pandemic. In fact, the more officials hired for heroin suppression work, the more are bribed, or worse, become distributors themselves. Thirty federal agents within the last eighteen months alone have been indicted for being directly involved in the heroin (i.e. junk) trade" (43). Ashley (1972, 136) adds that the enforcement of narcotics prohibition "has created a business whose profits make the rum-running of the Prohibition Era appear bush league by comparison . . . [and] these profits have corrupted our police."

The international scope of narcotics and marijuana prohibition has resulted in corruption at the highest levels of governments. The intense enforcement within the United States and at the borders has exported the problems associated with prohibitions, especially corruption, to foreign countries. Ethan A. Nadelmann (1988) has noted that this high-level corruption in foreign countries is the direct result of drug-prohibition policies:

> Government officials ranging from common police officers to judges to cabinet ministers have been offered bribes many times their annual government salaries, and often for doing nothing more than looking the other way. In addition, the limits on what can be bought with corruption have evaporated. Supreme court judges, high-ranking police and military officers, and cabinet ministers are no longer above such things. The ultimate degree of corruption is when government officials take the initiative in perpetrating crimes. This has occurred not just in the major drug-producing countries but throughout the continent as well. No country, from Cuba to Chile, seems to be immune. (86–87)

Indeed, the number of countries affected by corruption because of drug-prohibition policies is substantial.[1]

The Cost of Corruption

Corruption imposes serious costs on society through its general effects and those on government and police organizations. By facili-

---

[1]Countries with significant prohibition-induced corruption include Venezuela, Colombia, Brazil, Peru, Bolivia, Panama, Cuba, Mexico, the Bahamas, Lebanon, Morocco, Turkey, Iraq, Iran, Afghanistan, Pakistan, the countries of Southeast Asia, Italy, France, Spain, and the United States. This list is not intended to be complete, nor is it in any particular order.

tating exchange in prohibited markets, corruption not only goes against the goals of prohibitions but also makes the reduction of consumption more difficult. Attempts to control corruption represent an additional cost of prohibition, and in places such as Hong Kong, strong corruption-control agencies have been shown to suppress political opposition groups and civil liberties. The existence of pervasive corruption results in a diminished respect for law in general, adding further to the problems of crime, productivity, and delinquency.

Several authors have considered the potential benefits of corruption. Dorothy H. Bracey (1976) and Herman Goldstein (1975) note that increased mutual interdependence, the ability to overcome bureaucratic red tape, and the desire of bribe takers to be considered good employees may reinforce the chain of command and may reduce organizational problems in corrupt police departments. Sisk (1982) notes that bribery reduces the cost of government by supplementing salaries. Indeed, an examination of the vast literature on corruption, particularly in developing countries, indicates that economists should consider bribery as a primary method of public finance alongside taxation, borrowing, and inflation. James M. Buchanan 1973 has noted that monopolies in illegal goods are socially preferable because monopolies restrict output in order to increase profits.

These "benefits" are, of course, more than offset by other considerations. Once a relationship is established between police officials and black-market monopolists, the police become responsive to the monopolist and are less responsive to the needs of the general public. The police officials may even become actively involved in the management and maintenance of the monopoly. The police may condone or participate in violent crimes against new entrants or third parties in the pursuit of maintaining the monopoly and its profits. Further, the police may act to extend the monopoly or to create new ones. As Sisk (1982) concludes: "If the true consequences of such laws, police corruption, and the possibility of using taxes to impose costs on these activities were well publicized, supporters of such laws could no longer hide behind a shield of morality" (403).

Corruption leads police officials either to break the laws they are hired to enforce or to neglect their duties in favor of more profitable activities of supporting the monopoly. Therefore, the corruption resulting from prohibition not only reduces the effectiveness of prohibition, it may also cause an increase in the (victimless) crimes it was supposed to reduce and may increase crimes of a serious nature.

6

The Repeal of Prohibition

It seems certain, therefore, that the Eighteenth Amendment
cannot be repealed, in whole or in part.
—(Irving Fisher, *Prohibition Still at Its Worst*)

The certainty Irving Fisher spoke of concerning the repeal of alcohol prohibition was also true of the first seventy-five years of narcotic prohibition. Repeal is only considered a viable option after all other measures have failed. Repeal and legalization have now come back into consideration, but they are still far from representing the views of the majority of the public.[1]

The repeal of prohibition is a radical proposal only in the sense that it goes to the root of the matter. The "matter" in this case is some combination of the failure of prohibition to address the problems of drug use and the negative results that prohibitions create. It is not radical in the sense that it has never been tried, would be unusual in content or results, or would represent some form of communism. Alcohol and tobacco prohibitions have been repealed and similar prohibitions have been repealed in other countries. In fact, the eventual repeal of the current prohibition is quite likely; the interesting and important question is, what will replace them?

A number of alternative policy regimes have been proposed to replace prohibition. Most of these suggestions involve some combination of government and market control. A likely scenario is that

---

[1] During the late 1970s, a substantial portion of the population supported the decriminalization of marijuana, and the Carter administration seriously considered this possibility. The fiasco that overturned the movement is described by Patrick Anderson 1981.

after repeal (first for marijuana, then narcotics) the products would simply be governed by existing interventionist measures. For example, narcotics would become a "by prescription only" drug and marijuana would be regulated and taxed like alcohol and tobacco. This would be a simple and politically feasible option.

While politically feasible and preferable to current conditions, such a solution suffers two important defects. First, interventionist measures were found to be politically unstable for products consumed by a minority of the electorate. This instability is due in part to the second defect of interventionism: its inability to correct true social problems and its tendency to create new ones.

Based on the results of my research, legalization is the option considered last but most likely to succeed. *Decriminalization* (the reduction in criminal status or regulation of an activity or product) as a substitute for prohibition is desired primarily as a politically expedient transition mechanism to *legalization* (to make an activity legal and subject to the normal market and legal constraints). As W. H. Hutt (1971) suggests, political viability should be the last consideration of the policy analyst, if it is to be considered at all.

Many of the early studies of prohibition were biased and flawed. The level of economic analysis and the methodology employed were simply inadequate to the task of studying prohibition and black markets. Early students of prohibition produced little in the way of an economic theory of prohibition.

The market-process approach to government intervention provides a general framework of analysis that, when applied to prohibition, yields valuable theoretical insights. Contributions from economics, history, sociology, and criminology support this market-process perspective.

History reveals that prohibitions were established on rent-seeking grounds. The original intent of temperance reformers was public spirited, but these reformers turned to political solutions, and temperance evolved into a political movement. The adoption of prohibitions was shown to be the goal of a coalition of politicians and bureaucrats, rent seeking on the part of professional and religious groups, and basic prejudice against certain minority and immigrant groups, such as Mexicans and blacks.

The first result derived from the market-process approach is an understanding of the undiscovered discovery process. Policymakers adopt prohibition policies in part because of their (and their constituents') failure to recognize the market's ability to correct for imperfections. The market does not make such corrections perfectly or instantaneously (as indicated by the model of perfect competition), and this is the case with prohibition. Temperance advocates were impatient, so they resorted to politically based solutions, eventually turning to prohibition.

The unsimulated discovery process (bureaucracy) plays a role in both the adoption of prohibition and its inability to achieve desired results. The bureaucratic nature of government is incompatible with successful experimentation, innovation, and entrepreneurship. Bureaucracy has no clear and objective mechanism for recognizing efficient solutions. Innovation and evaluation are further hampered in bureaucracy by the need to institute system-wide policies and rules.

The bureaucracy also hampers the market's ability to produce desired solutions. For example, Sam Peltzman (1974) found that regulation stifled the "discovery process" in the pharmaceutical industry. The stifling of discovery in the market is more severe under prohibition than under regulation because prohibition negates the market, whereas regulation merely hampers it. Prohibition's stifling of the discovery process extends to other areas, such as product quality, the availability of complements and substitutes, and product information.

Information is distorted by prohibition in many ways. In the infamous case of the nineteenth-century patent drugs, state prohibition laws and exemptions for patent medicines containing opiates resulted in the widespread addiction of unsuspecting consumers. Individuals seeking relief from addiction or attempting to avoid addiction were duped by the coexistence of state prohibition laws and the availability of legal narcotic preparations.

While such bureaucratic miscalculation might be treated as ignorance or the result of rent-seeking behavior, it must nonetheless be seen as a normal and predictable result of interventionist policies. A more recent example is the requirement of warning labels on cigarette packages; the unintended effect was an increase in consumption by teenagers of such alternative tobacco products as chewing and snuffing tobacco, for which warning labels were not required.

The "wholly superfluous discovery process" is a category of results that was found particularly where the black market supplants the legal market. In black markets, the incentives of suppliers tend to be completely dominated by the effects of prohibition. Crime and higher-potency drugs are the types of effects brought about by the new profit opportunities provided by prohibition. The new profit opportunities not only made prohibition more difficult to enforce, they produced results that ran counter to the goals of prohibition.

The question of the potency and quality of products has important implications for the possibility of effective prohibition. As more resources are devoted to the enforcement of prohibition (or penalties are increased) suppliers resort to increasing potency, higher-potency types of drugs and reduction in product quality, product attributes (such as safety and information), and complementary goods (such as needles, filters, and antidotes). These adjustments not only make prohibition more difficult to enforce, they produce results which are antithetical to the goals of prohibition. Most important, changes in potency and product quality counter the argument that the goals of prohibition are achieved because a smaller quantity is consumed.

The issues of crime and corruption have negative implications for the possibility of effective prohibition. As more resources are devoted to prohibition, the price of the prohibited product increases. This causes the real income of illegal-drug users to decline and creates profit opportunities for suppliers and public officials. As a result, total crime and corruption increase under prohibition. Crime and corruption make the enforcement of prohibition more difficult because crime increases the income of drug consumers and corruption decreases the costs to suppliers. Crime also increases as enforcement resources are diverted to prohibition. Prohibition-induced crime and corruption also exacerbate the problems that prohibition hopes to solve. Like potency and product quality, crime and corruption act as vents for avoiding the intentions of prohibition and make it more difficult and costly. The increases in crime and corruption due to prohibition hinder the attainment of effective prohibition.

IS EFFECTIVE PROHIBITION POSSIBLE?

It is possible to enact prohibitions under virtually any form of government, and in fact, prohibitions have been enacted by almost every presently existing national government and the United Nations. It is also now generally agreed that complete prohibition is impossible to achieve, except in the most limited sense (where there is little or no existing demand for the product or where there exist near-perfect legal substitutes). The political possibility of enacting prohibition and the impossibility of achieving complete prohibition, however, are not the issues raised here.

The debate about prohibition has centered on the costs and benefits of prohibition. The intended benefits of prohibition all depend on decreasing the quantity consumed. The costs of prohibition include the explicit cost of law enforcement and implicit costs, such as the opportunity cost of the courts and prisons, and the increased crime and corruption that result from prohibition. The cost of prohibition has been shown to be a function of the resources devoted to the enforcement of prohibition and to be greater than previously thought. An important but neglected cost is the stifling effect that prohibition has on the market-discovery process.

The case against prohibition presented here does not rest mainly on the cost of prohibition outweighing the benefits, but rather on the absence of benefits as the decrease in quantity is more than offset by higher potency, more dangerous types of drugs, and increased crime and corruption. Just as consumers have demonstrated that they will pay black-market prices for prohibited goods, however, supporters of prohibition have demonstrated that they will vote for increasing amounts of resources to enforce prohibition. This support continues despite the public's recognition of the inability of these increased resources to bring about desirable results.

Randy Barnett (1987, 73–76) notes that Americans have become psychologically addicted to drug laws. He also realizes that other drug-law users, such as politicians, bureaucrats, researchers, and academics, ignore the costs of prohibition because of their "economic dependence" on such laws. Thomas S. Szasz (1985, 342–45 and elsewhere) makes the argument that the United States has become a therapeutic state (union of state and medicine), similar to the theocratic state. In a therapeutic state the interests of government and medicine dominate any concern about the costs of prohibitions.

The benefits of prohibition (if there are any) must be viewed by the economists as just as subjective as the value of lollipops or the Mona Lisa. Due to its political nature and a lack of market valuations, the value of prohibition simply cannot be definitively and accurately demonstrated. In fact, the current prohibitions were not and never have been subject to a popular vote. Policy experts and pollsters can provide no more than "best guesses" produced by politically motivated cost-benefit analysis and opinion surveys.

Fortunately, a more basic level of analysis is available for the economist to consider—the existence, rather than the perception or amount, of benefits. The neglect of this fundamental level of analysis can be attributed largely to the reduction in quantity demanded that is expected from prohibition and to the fact that the benefits of prohibition are perceived to be a function of the quantity consumed. If prohibition increases price, other things equal, there must be benefits. While prohibition certainly does increase price, it also increases potency and decreases quality. While not crucial to this argument, many, including Brecher (1972), have argued that prohibition increases the demand for and consumption of the prohibited product.

With regard to quantity consumed, increase in potency is a major factor in maintaining the real quantity-consumed constant. As to the quality of the product, it is greatly diminished by prohibition. The combination of increased potency and decreased quality makes the consumption of the product more dangerous and possibly more addictive. The substitution of more dangerous types of drugs has also been found to be a predictable effect of increased enforcement. Prohibition will deter some occasional users of a product but is unlikely to deter consumers who have an addiction to the prohibited good.[2] Those who do curtail their consumption of prohibited drugs can easily substitute legal drugs, intoxicants, and narcotics.[3]

Prohibition does not eliminate access to the product and does not discourage the very type of consumption it was designed to discourage. Therefore, the argument that increased price reduces quantity consumed and therefore produces benefits has yet to be established either in theory or in fact. The quantity of drugs captured by law

---

[2] Addicts and heavy users often do eventually end their use of addictive or harmful drugs, but this termination has mainly been attributed to aging or maturing rather than to higher prices or imprisonment.

[3] Prohibition of certain drugs increases the sales of legal intoxicants such as alcohol. This substitution cannot be considered socially beneficial even without making the dubious comparison of the harmful or potentially harmful effects of drugs produced in the market to drugs produced in the black market.

enforcement is not a benefit of prohibition; it is merely a cost of doing business in the black market.

Prohibition appears to be helpless in decreasing demand or in preventing increases in demand. Government statistics indicate that the consumption of marijuana has decreased or leveled off in recent years. Still, it would be a mistake to declare this a benefit of prohibition and increased enforcement. First, the statistics themselves are in some doubt. Marijuana production has increased in small plots and indoors, where information on production is difficult to ascertain, and the potency of marijuana has continued to increase. Potency-adjusted consumption of marijuana may have increased. Even if a decrease in consumption has occurred, it would not be a benefit of prohibition; quite the contrary. Government estimates of consumption have shown that the street price of marijuana has increased, the price of cocaine has decreased, and the consumption of cocaine has increased. These estimates are consistent with a shift in demand between substitute products, which is predictable as a result of increased enforcement.

In this book I have established the *possibility* of the impossibility of prohibition. The stronger case—that effective prohibition *is* impossible (that is, without any benefit)—is difficult to demonstrate and is subject to a variety of criticisms. A general criticism of the impossibility thesis is that all the possible benefits were not considered. Indeed, one point raised concerning the effects of prohibition is that not all the possible ramifications of prohibition may be known or apparent to either the examiner or the policymaker. For example, it could be claimed that prohibition can reduce expenditures on a certain product under certain conditions.[4]

---

[4] It could then be argued that these decreased expenditures outweigh total costs and therefore effective prohibition is possible. Prohibition can reduce expenditures in only the most extreme and restrictive sense, however—that is, where demand is elastic and does not result in the substitution of other intoxicants. Most estimates of expenditures show that total expenditures during prohibition remain the same or increase from what would have been spent in the absence of prohibition. The first full year of National Alcohol Prohibition (1921) appears to be the only documented case of reduced expenditures (Warburton 1932, 170–71). He also noted, however, that "we must conclude that the adoption of national prohibition has failed to reduce the use of alcoholic beverages and has increased the sum spent on them." No one argues that

In this book I have examined all the (well-intentioned) known arguments for prohibition. Many of these arguments I have explored in great detail. None of them can be shown to have demonstrated viable benefits, and no empirical study has been found to negate this conclusion adequately. Many of the arguments I examined here need further inspection and elaboration.

The termination of prohibition does not necessarily follow from the theoretical conclusion that prohibition is effectively impossible. Two important questions must first be raised. First, given the costs that prohibition has imposed, is termination a reasonable course to follow? For example, prohibition has resulted in higher-potency products and new, more dangerous drugs. Would repeal result in even higher potencies and more dangerous drugs? Second, despite a lack of benefits, might not prohibition still provide value? For instance, if we assume that the market does not induce improvements and the costs of prohibition can be ignored, might not prohibition provide value to society by taking a position (although futile) on an important issue? While these two questions do not deal directly with the economic results of prohibition, they are important policy considerations.

ALTERNATIVE POLICY REGIMES

Much of the debate about prohibition concerns how to enforce it and how much to spend on enforcement. I argue that enforcement cannot achieve the public-spirited goals of prohibition and that more resources will only make a bad situation worse.

Alternatives to prohibition involve some measure of decriminalization. Policy options such as nationalization (government drugstores), licensing requirements, price controls, taxation, regulation, a variety of maintenance programs, quarantine, education, and rehabilitation would be improvements over prohibition. Many of these reforms are questionable, however, in terms of their effectiveness, their ability to produce long-term solutions, and their stability as

---

prohibition has reduced total expenditures on heroin, cocaine, or marijuana. In fact, it is well recognized that the national expenditure on products such as cocaine and marijuana are significantly higher with prohibition.

long-term public policy. These reforms have the additional liability of being specific to one prohibition, rather than being a general remedy for all prohibitions. Full legalization is an alternative to these interventionist reform measures. The major problems it poses are its political feasibility and stability.

Clague (1973) examined several strategies for dealing with heroin addiction, including prohibition, strict and permissive methadone maintenance programs, heroin maintenance, and quarantine. He then evaluated these schemes against seven criteria: amount of crime, number of addicts, well-being of addicts, police corruption, violation of civil liberties, legal deprivation of traditional liberties, and respect for law (in general). Based on his analysis, Clague ranked each scheme's performance on the seven criteria on a five-point scale.[5] He found that prohibition ranked last and heroin maintenance ranked the best.[6]

While heroin maintenance ranked the highest among the policies studied, Clague admits that for a variety of reasons, it is not "an ideal solution to the heroin problem" (1973, 267). In addition to maintaining addiction and several practical problems, government-sponsored maintenance programs involve taxpayer subsidies to addicts. This option creates resentment on the part of antidrug taxpayers and therefore political instability.[7] John Kaplan (1983) also examined a

---

[5] Clague freely admits his ranking is highly subjective and that in two instances he is unable to assign an ordinal ranking. His rankings are based on the long-term effects of the policies and do not consider short-run adjustments or the relative weight of each criterion.

[6] He found that the quarantine scheme ranked high in several criteria but that serious problems in law, the Constitution, notions of justice, and increases in "resentment and alienation in many quarters" resulted in very low ranking in "legal deprivation of traditional liberties" and "respect for law." Therefore, one would have to place little or negative importance on matters of justice, liberty, and respect for the law in order to rank quarantine above heroin maintenance.

[7] Providing subsidies to drug addicts is just as abhorrent to certain taxpayers as providing taxpayer-subsidized abortions. Musto (1987, 64 and elsewhere) showed that the early narcotic-maintenance programs were "unwieldy and unpopular" and were quickly closed. In addition to creating resentment and costs to taxpayers, this policy tends to condone heroin use and reduces the perceived and real costs of addiction to the addict.

variety of policy options for heroin. He also found that heroin main-tenance and other options faced operational drawbacks and political obstacles.[8]

Moore (1973) suggested that a policy of heroin maintenance for addicts combined with prohibition would achieve price discrimination in the heroin market. Maintenance would reduce the costs of addiction to the addict and society, while prohibition would impose a greatly increased price on illegal heroin (over general prohibition) and therefore discourage experimentation with heroin. Moore's "highly speculative discussion" was not meant to demonstrate which policy was most desirable but rather was intended to investigate the determinants of effective price and, with extension, demand for heroin. In this sense, Moore's contribution is an important contribution to the a priori evaluation of various policies.

Fines have been suggested as an efficient substitute for imprisonment. If prohibition can be viewed as a form of price control, then fines could be substituted as a deterrent that would save prison resources. John R. Lott and Russel D. Roberts (1989) have examined this question and found that a legalization and price-control approach for traditional "victimless crimes" (for example, prohibitions) lacks the necessary incentives for effective enforcement. In addition, victimless crimes are difficult to monitor; the goods are highly mobile, a social stigma is attached to these goods, and the queuing or surpluses that result from price controls present special social problems. Therefore, what works in the enforcement of rent controls and minimum-wage laws does not work in the enforcement of prohibitions. Taxation is an often-suggested alternative to prohibition. Taxing marijuana is seen as a particularly viable option, but taxing opiates is not (Kaplan 1983, 150–51). The benefits of taxation include a reduction in crime and a deterrent to buying because of the higher cost, but the primary benefit is political. The revenue would make decriminalization more attractive to taxpayers and politicians. While the taxation option has much to recommend it, many of its beneficial aspects are reduced or eliminated as the tax

---

[8] It should be noted that the difficulties associated with "free availability" were based on a "greatly increased addiction rate" and the public health and personal aspects associated with an increased addiction rate.

rate increases.[9] High tax rates would maintain the black market, smuggling, crime, and corruption, and have little positive impact on drug abuse and therefore would create the preconditions for introducing prohibition. Even an ad potere tax has drawbacks, such as sending signals to potential consumers that low-potency products are safe to consume.

The repeal of Prohibition in 1933 set the stage for policy experimentation.[10] Some states remained dry, while others resorted to licensing requirements or state monopoly. The federal government employed taxes, tariffs, regulations, and license requirements. State governments imposed taxes and placed restrictions on the sale of alcohol. Regulations were placed on the potency of the product. For example, the potency of beer was limited to 3.2 percent in some states, although these regulations were primarily for taxation purposes. Additional interventions included age restrictions, advertising restrictions, local option, restrictions on the hours of sale, and price controls.[11] Although legalization has been an improvement over prohibition, these interventions and the prohibition of other intoxicants, such as marijuana and cocaine, have resulted in mediocre results at best (see Sylbing 1985, and Sylbing and Persoon 1985). One benefit of legalization is the development of social institutions that deal directly or indirectly with the problems of addiction and drug abuse, such as Alcoholics Anonymous (formed in the mid–1930s), which today claims more than one million members.[12]

THE FREE-MARKET SOLUTION

Prohibition is effectively impossible in the economic sense. Alternative policies, such as government-sponsored maintenance pro-

---

[9] See Rodney T. Smith 1976 on government's tendency to maximize net revenues and its impact on the alcohol industry.

[10] For a history of the repeal movement, see Kyvig 1979. For an unsympathetic view on the repeal movement, see Dobyns 1940.

[11] For a history of the plethora of policies enacted after repeal, see Harrison and Laine 1936.

[12] A great deal of this organization's success must be attributed to the anonymous status of its members. The organization *does not* advocate prohibition or severe restrictionism on the part of government to the problems of alcohol abuse.

grams, also exhibit problems but represent an improvement over prohibition. The free-market solution differs from these alternative policies in that it involves no government intervention.

The free market has traditionally been viewed as the cause rather than the cure for the problems of drug abuse. I maintain that the free-market solution involves voluntary choices of individuals within an environment of free entry, property rights, and a legal system. Entrepreneurs hire labor and purchase resources to produce, promote, and sell products to consumers. Consumers choose among diversified products in an attempt to maximize utility. Exchange results in gains to both parties and an efficient allocation of resources. Charitable and self-help groups form to solve social problems.

Prohibitionists would, of course, scoff at such a description as it applies to the market for drugs.[13] Indeed, the market as it has been described here is not perfect. It is characterized by risk and uncertainty. Mistakes, such as addiction or overdoses, will no doubt occur in any system. The competition and the discovery process that characterize the development of a market promote solutions to the problems of drug abuse that prohibition seeks to solve.

The free-market solution would have many benefits:

1. A competitive price would ultimately free up resources for the consumption of such goods as food, clothing, shelter, and medical care.

2. The profit motive would stimulate producers to introduce goods with characteristics that enhance consumer satisfaction. Deadly products that survive in black markets would be eliminated. Producers would compete by improving their products to meet the desires of consumers. The market for a particular drug, such as alcohol, marijuana, or aspirin would be characterized by diversified products.

3. As with any dangerous product, suppliers would prefer regular customers who are familiar with the product, thereby reducing

---

[13] Some critics of the market view it as "too practical," focusing only on consumers' or producers' direct interests, rather than on political (i.e., the majority's) interests. Other critics claim that the market solution is too "impractical," that it does not address the problems of consumers and producers, or that such a substitution is "politically impossible."

expenditures on marketing and their exposure to liability law. Suppliers would no longer enlist the services of minors to retail their products.

4. Information about product availability, price, and product quality would be available. Advertising would convey information about the unique features of a particular brand.

5. Producers would engage in product standardization, brand-name labeling, directions for use, product safety information, and so on.

6. The crime and corruption that result from prohibition, taxation, regulations, and other policy options would be eliminated.

7. Government expenditures on law enforcement, prisons, and courts could be reduced. Courts would not be as backlogged, prisons would be less crowded, and the police could concentrate resources on traditional crimes, such as murder, rape, and robbery. These changes might help promote respect for law and order.

8. Individuals would be directly responsible for their own use or nonuse of drugs. More resources and public attention could be devoted to education, treatment, maintenance, and rehabilitation.

9. Consumers would have access to the legal system to protect them against fraud and negligence on the part of the producer. Producers would no longer have to resort to violence to enforce contracts and ensure payments. Sales territories would be maintained by voluntary agreement rather than by violence.

10. Many of the products that have been prohibited have "legitimate" uses and were important products in the development of modern civilization. Legalization would allow for their use in these and other areas, and would promote general economic development.

This list covers many of the major benefits of the free-market solution. These benefits can be summarized as freeing up valuable resources, providing incentives for improvements, and eliminating the costs (both direct and unintended) of prohibition.

THE EXTENDED FREE-MARKET SOLUTION

The free-market solution as applied to one drug or all drugs would not achieve ideal results. Short-term adjustments to free-mar–

ket conditions involve substantial costs. Discovering techniques to avoid and cure addiction and to develop new institutions and safer products would all take time. In fact, achieving "solutions" to the use of addictive products may take generations, rather than months and years.

Extending the free-market solution to areas other than the immediate market for drugs would help in the development of such solutions. Circumstances such as war, poverty, discrimination, and a loss of economic opportunity are associated with drug abuse and addiction. Applying the market solution throughout the economy, or to such specific markets as insurance, medicine, housing, and labor, also allows opportunity for improvement. Some of the possible benefits of the extended free-market solution follow.

1. Market economies use resources efficiently and produce higher standards of living. Market economies are characterized by capital accumulation and lower time preferences (longer time horizons).
2. Removal of barriers to entry into the medical profession would reduce the costs of health care and treatment for addiction. Removal of government-subsidized medical care would place the entire cost of drug abuse on the abuser, rather than providing a subsidy for abuse.
3. Insurance companies and employers could control and discriminate against persons who abuse drugs, placing a direct and visible cost on drug users and abusers.
4. Economists have found that more economic discrimination occurs in nationalized and regulated industries and occupations. Removal of these barriers would create economic opportunities for the disfranchised.
5. War has been found to play an important role in creating and stimulating the problems of drug abuse (and prohibitions). The absence of war would likely decrease the probability of prohibitions.

The extended free-market solution is a complement to the free-market alternative to prohibition and an important component of the ultimate solution to the problems of drug abuse. Both policies share two shortcomings. First, neither would produce ideal or immediate solutions. In fact, some people other than bureaucrats and interest groups would be hurt by this change in policy: for example, black marketeers and certain politicians and government researchers. Prohibition, of course, is even further from solving the problems, and all policy changes involve short-term adjustments. Second, the prospects for such policies are rather limited. Substantive changes in policy are difficult at best, and when they do occur they are almost always a substitution of one form of government intervention for another. Political possibility is not a direct criterion of economic analysis or policy recommendations, however.

After a century of experimentation with prohibition, solutions to the problems of drug abuse still elude our policymakers. The political infeasibility of the free-market solution, or any policy, has not deterred some economists from incorporating that policy into their analyses or their advocacy of reform. The changes in public sentiment that have occurred in the early 1990s suggest that repeal of the prohibition on narcotics is likely, and that their relegalization is possible. As in many other cases, real solutions to serious problems may be found only at the root and may be solved only with a revolution of ideas and dramatic change.

References

Abel, Ernest L. 1980. *Marihuana: The First Twelve Thousand Years*. New York: Plenum Press.

Alchian, Armen, and William R. Allen. 1964. *University Economics*. Belmont, Calif.: Wadsworth.

Anderson, Gary M., and Robert D. Tollison. 1988. "Democracy, Interest Groups, and the Price of Votes." *Cato Journal* 8 (Spring/Summer): 51–70.

Anderson, Patrick. 1981. *High in America: The True Story Behind NORML and the Politics of Marijuana*. New York: Viking Press.

Andreano, Ralph, and John J. Siegfried, eds. 1980. *The Economics of Crime*. New York: Wiley.

Ashley, Richard. 1972. *Heroin: The Myths and Facts*. New York: St. Martins Press.

Astor, Gerald. 1971. *The New York Cops: An Informal History*. New York: Scribner.

Ault, Richard, and Robert B. Ekelund, Jr. 1988. "Habits in Economic Analysis: Veblen and the Neoclassicals." *History of Political Economy* 20 (Fall): 431–45.

Banfield, Edward. 1975. "Corruption as a Feature of Governmental Organization." *Journal of Law and Economics* 18 (December): 587–605.

Barthold, T. A., and H. M. Hochman. 1988. "Addiction as Extreme-Seeking." *Economic Inquiry* 26 (January): 89–106.

Barzel, Yoram. 1976. "An Alternative Approach to the Analysis of Taxation." *Journal of Political Economy* 84 (December): 1177–98.

Bassett, John Spenser. 1932. *A Short History of the United States: 1492–1929*. New York: Macmillan.

Becker, Gary S., 1962. "Irrational Behavior and Economic Theory." *Journal of Political Economy* 70 (February): 1–13.

_____.1963. "A Reply to I. Kirzner." *Journal of Political Economy* 71 (February): 82–83.

_____.1968. "Crime and Punishment: An Economic Approach." *Journal of Political Economy* 76 (March): 169–217.

_____.1987. "Should Drug Use Be Legalized?" *Business Week*, August 17, p. 22.

Becker, Gary S., and Kevin M. Murphy. 1988. "A Theory of Rational Addiction." *Journal of Political Economy* 96 (August): 675–700.

Becker, Gary S., and George J. Stigler. 1974. "Law Enforcement, Malfeasance, and Compensation of Enforcers." *Journal of Legal Studies* 3 (January): 1–18.

Becker, H. S. 1963. *Outsiders: Studies in the Sociology of Deviance*. New York: Free Press.

Benson, Bruce L., 1981. "A Note on Corruption by Public Officials: The Black Market for Property Rights." *Journal of Libertarian Studies* 5 (Summer): 305–11.

_____.1984. "Rent Seeking from a Property Rights Perspective, *Southern Economic Journal* 51 (October): 388–400.

_____.1988. "An Institutional Explanation for Corruption of Criminal Justice Officials." *Cato Journal* 8 (Spring/Summer): 139–63.

Benson, Bruce L., and John Baden. 1985. "The Political Economy of Governmental Corruption: The Logic of Underground Government." *Journal of Legal Studies* 14 (June): 391–410.

Benson, Bruce L., Iljoong Kim, David W. Rasmussen, and Thomas W. Zuehlke. 1990. "Is Property Crime Caused by Drug Use or by Drug Enforcement Policy?" Florida State University. Typescript.

Bentham, Jeremy. 1896. *Theory of Legislation*. London: Kegan Paul.

Bidinotto, Robert James. 1989. *Crime and Consequences*. Irvington-on-Hudson, N. Y.: Foundation for Economic Education.

Blake, John B., ed. 1970. *Conference on the History of Medicinal Drug Control*. Baltimore: Johns Hopkins University Press.

Blocker, Jack S. 1976. *Retreat from Reform: The Prohibition Movement in the United States, 1890–1913*. Westport, Conn.: Greenwood Press.

Bonger, W. A. 1916. *Criminality and Economic Conditions*. Boston: Little, Brown.

Bonnie, Richard J., and Charles Whitebread II. 1974. *The Marijuana Conviction: A History of Marijuana Prohibition in the United States*. Charlottesville: University of Virginia Press.

Boorstin, Daniel J. 1958. *The Americans: The Colonial Experience*. New York: Random House.

Bookstaber, Richard. 1976. "Risk and the Structure of the Black Market for Addictive Drugs." *American Economist*, Spring, 26–29.

Borcherding, T. E., and E. Silberg. 1978. "Shipping the Good Apples Out: The Alchian and Allen Theorem Reconsidered." *Journal of Political Economy* 86 (February): 131–38.

Bracey, Dorothy H. 1976. *A Functional Approach to Police Corruption*. New York: John Jay Press.

Brandstatter, A. F. 1962. "New Frontiers for the Police." *Police* 7 (November/December): 13–20.

Brecher, Edward M. 1972. *Licit and Illicit Drugs*. Boston: Little, Brown.

Brooks, J. E. 1952. *The Mighty Leaf: Tobacco through the Centuries*. Boston: Little, Brown.

Brown, George F., Jr., and Lester P. Silverman. 1974. "The Retail Price of Heroin: Estimation and Applications." *Journal of the American Statistical Association* 69, no. 347 (September): 595–606.

Bryce, James. 1910. *The American Commonwealth*. Vol. 2. New York: Macmillan.

Buchanan, James M. 1973. "A Defense of Organized Crime?" In *The Economics of Crime and Punishment*, edited by Simon Rottenberg, 119–32. Washington, D.C.: American Enterprise Institute.

_____.1986. "Politics and Meddlesome Preferences." In *Smoking and Society: Toward a More Balanced Assessment*, edited by Robert D. Tollison, 335–42. Lexington, Mass.: Lexington Books.

Buchanan, James M., and Gordon Tullock. 1965. *The Calculus of Consent: Logical Foundations of Constitutional Democracy*. Ann Arbor: University of Michigan Press.

Bureau of Prohibition. 1930. *The Value of Law Observance*. Washington, D.C.: Government Printing Office.

Burrow, James G. 1977. *Organized Medicine in the Progressive Era: The Move Towards Monopoly*. Baltimore: Johns Hopkins University Press.

Byrne, Frank L. 1969. *Prophet of Prohibition: Neal Dow and His Crusade*. Gloucester, Mass.: Peter Smith.

Cameron, Samuel. 1989. "A Subjectivist Perspective of the Economics of Crime." *Review of Austrian Economics* 3: 31–43. Lexington, Mass.: Lexington Books.

Cave, Jonathan A. K., and Peter Reuter. 1988. "The Interdictor's Lot: A Dynamic Model of the Market for Drug Smuggling Services." *A Rand Note*. February. N-2632-USDP. Santa Monica, Calif.: The Rand Corp.

Clague, Christopher. 1973. "Legal Strategies for Dealing with Heroin Addiction." *American Economic Review* 63 (May): 263–69.

Coats, A. W. 1987. "Simon Newton Patten." In *The New Palgrave: A Dictionary of Economics*, edited by John Eatwell, Murray Milgate, and Peter Newman, 3: 818–19. London: Macmillan.

Coffey, Thomas. 1975. *The Long Thirst: Prohibition in America, 1920–1933*. New York: Norton.

Cook, Philip J., and Gary A. Zarkin. 1985. "Crime and the Business Cycle." *Journal of Legal Studies* 14 (January): 115–28.

Courtwright, David T. 1982. *Dark Paradise: Opiate Addiction in America Before 1940*. Cambridge, Mass.: Harvard University Press.

Crawford, Gordon B., Peter Reuter, Karen Isaacson, and Patrick Murphy. 1988. "Simulation of Adaptive Response: A Model of Drug Interdiction." *A Rand Note*. February. N-2680-USDP. Santa Monica, Calif.: The Rand Corp.

Croce, Benedetto. 1953. "On the Economic Principle." *International Economic Papers, No. 3*. 172–79, 197–202. New York: Macmillan.

Dickson, Donald T. 1968. "Bureaucracy and Morality." *Social Problems*, 16: 143–56.

Dobyns, Fletcher. 1940. *The Amazing Story of Repeal: An Exposé of the Power of Propaganda*. Chicago: Willett, Clark.

Dolan, Edwin G., and John C. Goodman. 1989. *Economics of Public Policy*. 4th edition. St. Paul, Minn.: West Publishing.

Duchaine, Nina. 1979. *The Literature of Police Corruption*. Vol. 2: *A Selected, Annotated Bibliography*. New York: John Jay Press.

Ehrlich, Isaac. 1973. "Participation in Illegitimate Activities: A Theoretical and Empirical Investigation." *Journal of Political Economy* 81 (August): 521–64.

_____.1975. "The Deterrent Effect of Capital Punishment: A Question of Life and Death." *American Economic Review* 65 (June): 397–417.

Ekelund, Robert B., Jr., and David S. Saurman. 1988. *Advertising and the Market Process*. San Francisco: Pacific Institute.

Ekelund, Robert B., Jr., and Robert D. Tollison. 1988. *Economics*. 2d ed. Glenview, Ill.: Scott, Foresman.

Eldridge, W. B. 1967. *Narcotics and the Law: A Critique of the American Experiment in Narcotic Drug Control*. 2d ed. Chicago: University of Chicago Press.

ElSohly, M. A., and Abel, C. T. 1988. "Quarterly Report of the Potency Monitoring Project." National Institute on Drug Abuse Marijuana Project, University of Mississippi, January–March.

Erickson, Edward. 1969. "The Social Costs of the Discovery and Suppression of the Clandestine Distribution of Heroin." *Journal of Political Economy* 17 (July/August): 484–86.

Faulkner, Harold Underwood. 1924. *American Economic History*. New York: Harper and Brothers.

Feenstra, Robert C. 1988. "Quality Change under Trade Restraints in Japanese Autos." *Quarterly Journal of Economics* 103 (February): 131–46.

Feldman, Herman. 1930. *Prohibition: Its Economic and Industrial Aspects*. New York: Appleton.

Ferdinand, Theodore N. 1967. "The Criminal Patterns of Boston since 1849." *American Journal of Sociology* 73: 84–99.

Fernandez, Raul A. 1969. "The Clandestine Distribution of Heroin, Its Discovery and Suppression: A Comment." *Journal of Political Economy* 77 (July/August): 487–88.

_____.1971. *Estimating Benefits for the Rehabilitation of Heroin Addicts*. Cambridge, Mass: N.P.

_____.1973. "The Problem of Heroin Addiction and Radical Political Economy." *American Economic Review* 63, no. 2 (May): 257–62.

Fisher, Irving. 1918. Abstract of "Some Contributions of the War to Our Knowledge of Money and Prices." *American Economic Review* 8 (March): 257–58.

_____.1919. "Economists in Public Service." (Annual Address of the President) *American Economic Review* 9 (March): 5–21.

_____.1922. *The Making of Index Numbers*. New York: Houghton Mifflin.

_____.1927. *Prohibition at Its Worst*. Rev. ed. New York: Alcohol Information Committee.

_____.1928. *Prohibition Still at Its Worst*. New York: Alcohol Information Committee.

_____.1930. *The "Noble Experiment."* New York: Alcohol Information Committee.

Fisher, Irving, et al. 1927. "The Economics of Prohibition." *American Economic Review: Supplement* 17 (March): 5–10.

Fisher, Irving Norton. 1956. *My Father, Irving Fisher*. New York: Comet Press.

Formisano, Ronald P. 1971. *The Birth of Mass Political Parties: Michigan, 1827–1861*. Princeton: Princeton University Press.

Fort, Joel. 1969. *The Pleasure Seekers*. New York: Grove Press.

Fox, Daniel M. 1967. *The Discovery of Abundance: Simon N. Patten and the Transformation of Social Theory*. Ithaca, N.Y.: Cornell University Press.

Friedman, Milton. 1972. "Prohibition and Drugs." *Newsweek*, May 1.

_____.1989. "An Open Letter to Bill Bennett." *Wall Street Journal*, September 7.

Friedman, Milton, and Rose Friedman. 1980. *Free to Choose: A Personal Statement*. New York: Harcourt Brace Jovanovich.

_____.1984. *Tyranny of the Status Quo*. New York: Harcourt Brace Jovanovich.

Gallagher, Winifred. 1986. "The Looming Menace of Designer Drugs." *Discover*, August, 24–35.

Gienapp, William E. 1987. *The Origins of the Republican Party, 1852–1856*. New York: Oxford University Press.

Goldstein, Herman. 1975. *Police Corruption: A Perspective on Its Nature and Control*. New York: Police Foundation.

Goode, Erich. 1972. *Drugs in American Society*. New York: Knopf.

Gould, John P., and Joel Segall. 1968. "The Substitution Effects of Transportation Costs." *Journal of Political Economy* 77 (January/February): 130–37.

Grimes, Alan P. 1967. *The Puritan Ethic and Woman Suffrage*. New York: Oxford University Press.

Haller, Mark H. 1970. "Urban Crime and Criminal Justice: The Chicago Case." *Journal of American History* 57: 619–35.

Hampel, Robert L. 1982. *Temperance and Prohibition in Massachusetts: 1813–1852*. Ann Arbor: UMI Research Press.

Harris, Jeffrey E. 1980. "Taxing Tar and Nicotine." *American Economic Review* 70 (June): 300–311.

Harrison, Leonard V., and Elizabeth Laine. 1936. *After Repeal: A Study of Liquor Control Administration*. New York: Harper and Brothers.

Hayek, F. A. 1937. "Economics and Knowledge." *Economica* 4 (February): 33–54.

_____.[1944] 1977. *The Road to Serfdom*. Chicago: University of Chicago Press.

_____.1945. "The Use of Knowledge in Society." *American Economic Review* 35(September): 519–30.

_____.1961. "The *Non Sequitur* of the 'Dependence Effect.' " *Southern Economic Journal* 27 (April): 346–48.

Helmer, John. 1975. *Drugs and Minority Oppression*. New York: Seabury Press.

Henry, Andrew F., and James F. Short, Jr. 1954. *Suicide and Homicide: Some Economic, Sociological, and Psychological Aspects of Aggression*. New York: Free Press.

Himmelstein, Jerome L. 1983. *The Strange Career of Marijuana: Politics and Ideology of Drug Control in America*. Westport, Conn.: Greenwood Press.

Hu, T. Y. 1950. *The Liquor Tax in the United States, 1791–1947: A History of the*

Internal Revenue Taxes Imposed on Distilled Spirits by the Federal Government.
New York: Columbia University Press.

Hutt, W. H. 1971. *Politically Impossible . . . ?* London: Institute of Economic
Affairs.

Ippolitio, Richard A., Dennis R. Murphy, and Donald Sant. 1979. *Staff Report
on Consumer Responses to Cigarette Health Information.* Washington, D.C.: Federal Trade Commission.

Jensen, Richard. 1971. *The Winning of the Midwest: Social and Political Conflict,
1888–1896.* Chicago: University of Chicago Press.

_____.1983. *Grass Root Politics: Parties, Issues, and Voters, 1854–1983.* Westport,
Conn.: Greenwood Press.

Johnson, B. D., P. J. Goldstein, E. Preble, J. Schmeidler, D. S. Lipton, B.
Spunt, and T. Miller. 1985. *Taking Care of Business: The Economics of Crime and
Heroin Abusers.* Lexington, Mass.: Lexington Books.

Johnson, Terry R. 1978. "Additional Evidence on the Effect of Alternative
Taxes on Cigarette Prices." *Journal of Political Economy* 86, no. 2, pt. 1.
(April): 325–28.

Johnson, W. E. 1917. *The Federal Government and the Liquor Traffic.* 2d ed. Wester-
ville, Ohio: American Issue Publishing Co.

Kaplan, John. 1983. *The Hardest Drug: Heroin and Public Policy.* Chicago: University of Chicago Press.

Kauffman, Reginald W. 1923. *The Real Story of a Bootlegger.* New York: Boni and
Liveright.

Kessel, Rubin A. 1958. "Price Discrimination in Medicine." *Journal of Law and
Economics* 1:20.

_____.1970. "The AMA and the Supply of Physicians." Symposium on Health
Care, Part 1. *Law and Contemporary Problems.*

_____.1972. "Higher Education and the Nation's Health: A Review of the
Carnegie Commission Report on Medical Education." *Journal of Law and
Economics* 15 (April): 115.

_____.1974. "Transfused Blood, Serum Hepatitis, and the Coase Theorem."
Journal of Law and Economics 17 (October): 265.

Key, V. O. 1958. *Politics, Parties, and Pressure Groups.* 4th ed. New York: Crowell.

Kirzner, Israel M. 1962. "Rational Action and Economic Theory." *Journal of
Political Economy* 71 (August): 380–85.

_____.1963. "Rejoinder." *Journal of Political Economy* 71 (February): 84–85.

_____.1973. *Competition and Entrepreneurship.* Chicago: University of Chicago
Press.

_____.1976. *Economic Point of View.* Kansas City: Sheed and Ward.

_____.1979. *Perception, Opportunity, and Profit: Studies in the Theory of Entrepre-
neurship.* Chicago: University of Chicago Press.

_____.1985. *Discovery and the Capitalist Process.* Chicago: University of Chicago
Press.

Klein, Benjamin, and Keith Leffler. 1981. "The Role of Market Forces in Assur-
ing Contractual Performance." *Journal of Political Economy* 89 (August):
615–41.

Kleinman, Mark A. R. 1989. *Marijuana: Costs of Abuse, Costs of Control.* Westport, Conn.: Greenwood Press.

Kleppner, Paul. 1979. *The Third Electoral System, 1853–1892: Parties, Voters, and Political Cultures.* Chapel Hill: University of North Carolina Press.

_____.1982. *Who Voted? The Dynamics of Electoral Turnout, 1870–1980.* New York: Praeger.

_____.1987. *Continuity and Change in Electoral Politics, 1893–1928.* Westport, Conn.: Greenwood Press.

Koren, John. 1899. *The Economic Aspects of the Liquor Traffic.* New York: Committee of Fifty.

Krout, John Allen. 1925. *The Origins of Prohibition.* New York: Knopf.

Kunnes, Richard. 1972. *The American Heroin Empire: Power, Profits, and Politics.* New York: Dodd, Mead.

Kyvig, David E. 1979. *Repealing National Prohibition.* Chicago: University of Chicago Press.

_____, ed. 1985. *Law, Alcohol, and Order: Perspectives on National Prohibition.* Westport, Conn.: Greenwood Press.

Lancaster, Kelvin J. 1966. "A New Approach to Consumer Theory." *Journal of Political Economy* 74 (April): 158–67.

Lane, Roger. 1968. "Crime and Criminal Statistics in Nineteenth-Century Massachusetts." *Journal of Social History* 2 (Winter): 156–63.

Lang, Alan R. 1983. "Addictive Personality: A Viable Construct?" In *Commonalities in Substance Abuse and Habitual Behavior,* ed. Peter K. Levinson, Dean R. Gerstein, and Deborah R. Maloff, 157–235. Lexington, Mass.: Lexington Books.

Lavine, Emanuel H. 1936. *Cheese It—The Cops!* New York: Vanguard Press.

Lindsey, C. M. 1976. "A Theory of Government Enterprise." *Journal of Political Economy* 84, No. 5: 1061–77.

Little, Arthur D. 1967. "Drug Abuse and Law Enforcement." *A Report of the President's Commission on Law Enforcement and Administration of Justice.* January 18. Unpublished.

Lott, John R., and Russel D. Roberts. 1989. "Why Comply: One-Sided Enforcement of Price Controls and Victimless Crime Laws." *Journal of Legal Studies* 18 (June): 403–14.

McDonald, Lynn. 1976. *The Sociology of Law and Order.* Boulder, Colo.: Westview Press.

_____.1982. "Theory and Evidence of Rising Crime in the Nineteenth Century." *British Journal of Sociology* 33 (September): 404–20.

McKenzie, R. B., and G. Tullock. 1989. *The Best of the New World of Economics.* 5th ed. Homewood, Ill.: Richard D. Irwin.

Michaels, Robert J. 1987. "The Market for Heroin before and after Legalization." In *Dealing with Drugs: Consequences of Government Control,* ed. Ronald Hamowy, 289–326. Lexington, Mass.: Heath.

_____."Addiction, Compulsion, and the Technology of Consumption." *Economic Enquiry* 26 (January): 75–88.

Mills, James. 1986. *The Underground Empire: Where Crime and Governments Embrace.* New York: Doubleday.

Mises, Ludwig von. [1929] 1977. *A Critique of Interventionism.* New Rochelle, N.Y.: Arlington House.

———.[1936] 1951. *Socialism: An Economic and Sociological Analysis.* Translated by J. Kahane. London: Johnathan Cape.

———.[1944] 1969. *Bureaucracy.* New Rochelle, N.Y.: Arlington House.

———.[1949] 1977. *Human Action.* New Haven: Yale University Press.

Monkkonen, Eric H. 1981. "A Disorderly People? Urban Order in the Nineteenth and Twentieth Centuries." *Journal of American History* 68 (December): 539–59.

Moore, Mark H. 1973. "Policy Towards Heroin Use in New York City." Ph.D. diss., Harvard University.

———.1973. "Policies to Achieve Discrimination on the Effective Price of Heroin." *American Economic Review* 63 (May): 270–77.

———.1976. "Anatomy of the Heroin Problem: An Exercise in Problem Definition." *Policy Analysis* 2, no. 4 (Fall): 639–62.

———.1977. *Buy and Bust: The Effective Regulation of an Illicit Market in Heroin.* Lexington, Mass.: Lexington Books.

Morgan, H. Wayne. 1974. *Yesterday's Addicts: American Society and Drug Abuse, 1865–1920.* Norman: University of Oklahoma Press.

Musto, David F. 1987. *The American Disease: Origins of Narcotic Control.* New York: Oxford University Press.

Nadelmann, Ethan A. 1988. "U.S. Drug Policy: A Bad Export." *Foreign Policy* 70 (Spring): 83–108.

National Institute on Drug Abuse, Drug Abuse Warning Network. 1981–84. *Annual Data Report.* Statistical series, series 1, no. 3. Washington, D.C.: U.S. Bureau of Justice.

Nelli, Humbert S. 1985. "American Syndicate Crime: A Legacy of Prohibition." In *Law, Alcohol, and Order: Perspectives on National Prohibition*, edited by David E. Kyvig, 123–38. Westport, Conn.: Greenwood Press.

Newcomb, Simon. [1886] 1966. *Principles of Political Economy.* New York: Augustus M. Kelley.

Niskanen, William. 1971. *Bureaucracy and Representative Government.* Chicago: Aldine-Atherton.

———.1975. "Bureaucrats and Politicians." *Journal of Law and Economics* 18 (December): 617–44.

North, Gary. 1988. *Puritan Economic Experiments.* Fort Worth, Tex.: Institute for Christian Economics.

Odegard, Peter H. [1928] 1966. *Pressure Politics: The Story of the Anti-Saloon League.* New York: Octagon Books.

———, ed. 1960. *Religion and Politics.* New Brunswick, N.J.: The Egleton Institute of Politics, Rutgers University.

Oliver, F. E. 1872. "The Use and Abuse of Opium." Boston: Wright and Potter. (Pp. 162–77 reprinted in H. Wayne Morgan, *Yesterday's Addicts: American*

Society and Drug Abuse, 1865–1920 [Norman: University of Oklahoma Press, 1974], 43–52.)

Ostrowski, James. 1989. "Thinking about Drug Legalization." *Policy Analysis* 121 (May 25): 1–64. Washington, D.C.: Cato Institute.

Palmer, Stanley H. *Police and Protest in England and Ireland, 1780–1850.* New York: Cambridge University Press.

Pandiani, John A. 1982. "The Crime Control Corps: An Invisible New Deal Program." *British Journal of Sociology* 33 (September): 348–58.

Patten, Simon N. [1885] 1968. *The Premises of Political Economy: Being a Re-Examination of Certain Fundamental Principles of Economic Science.* New York: Augustus M. Kelley.

_____.[1890]. 1973. *The Economic Basis for Protectionism.* Lippincott. New York: Arno Press.

_____.1891. "The Economic Basis of Prohibition." *Annals of the American Academy of Political and Social Sciences,* July, 60–66.

_____.1924. *Essays in Economic Theory.* Edited by Rexford Tugwell. New York: Knopf.

Peltzman, Sam. 1974. *Regulation of Pharmaceutical Innovation: The 1962 Amendments.* Washington, D.C.: American Enterprise Institute.

Phares, Donald. 1973. "The Simple Economics of Heroin and Organizing Policy." *Journal of Drug Issues* 3 (Spring): 186–200.

Pyle, David J. 1983. *The Economics of Crime and Law Enforcement.* New York: Macmillan.

Reed, Lear B. 1941. *Human Wolves.* Kansas City, Missouri: Brown, White, Lowell.

Reuter, Peter. 1983. *Disorganized Crime: The Economics of the Visible Hand.* Cambridge, Mass.: MIT Press.

Reuter, Peter, Gordon Crawford, and Jonathan Cave. 1988. "Sealing the Borders: The Effects of Increased Military Participation in Drug Interdiction." *A Rand Note.* January. R-3594-USDP. Santa Monica, Calif.: The Rand Corp.

Reuter, Peter, Robert MacCoun, Patrick Murphy, Allan Abrahamse, and Barbara Simon. 1990. "Money from Crime: A Study of the Economics of Drug Dealing in Washington, D.C." *A Rand Note.* June. R-3894-RF. Santa Monica, Calif.: The Rand Corp.

Roback, Jennifer. 1989. "Racism as Rent Seeking." *Economic Inquiry* 27 (October): 661–83.

Rose-Ackerman, Susan. 1975. "The Economies of Corruption." *Journal of Public Economics* 4:187.

_____.1978. *Corruption: A Study in Political Economy.* New York: Academic Press.

Rosenstone, Stephen J., Roy L. Behr, and Edward H. Lazarus. 1984. *Third Parties in America: Citizen Response to Major Party Failure.* Princeton: Princeton University Press.

Rothbard, Murray N. 1970. *Power and Market: Government and the Economy.* Menlo Park, Calif.: Institute for Humane Studies.

_____.1989. "World War I as Fulfillment: Power and the Intellectuals." *Journal of Libertarian Studies* 9 (Winter): 81–125.

Rottenberg, Simon, 1968. "The Clandestine Distribution of Heroin, Its Discovery and Suppression." *Journal of Political Economy* 76 (January/February): 78–90.

_____, ed. 1973. *The Economics of Crime and Punishment*. Washington, D.C.: American Enterprise Institute.

Rubin, Paul H. 1980. "The Economics of Criminal Activity." In *The Economics of Crime*, edited by Ralph Andreano and John J. Siegfried, 13–26. New York: Wiley.

Sait, Edward G. 1939. *American Parties and Elections*. New York: Appleton-Century.

Schecter, Leonard and William R. Phillips. 1973. *On the Pad; the Underworld and Its Corrupt Police: Confessions of a Cop on the Take*. New York: Putnam.

Silbey, Joel H. 1967. *The Transformation of American Politics, 1840–1860*. Englewood Cliffs, N.J.: Prentice-Hall.

_____.1973. *Political Ideology and Voting Behavior in the Age of Jackson*. Englewood Cliffs, N.J.: Prentice-Hall.

Silbey, Joel H., Allan G. Bogue, and William H. Flanigan, eds. 1978. *The History of American Electoral Behavior*. Princeton, N.J.: Princeton University Press.

Simpson, Anthony E. 1977. *The Literature of Police Corruption*. Vol. 1: *A Guide to Bibliography and Theory*. New York: John Jay Press.

Sisk, David E. 1982. "Police Corruption and Criminal Monopoly: Victimless Crimes." *Journal of Legal Studies* 11 (June): 395–403.

Sloman, Larry. 1979. *Reefer Madness: The History of Marijuana in America*. Indianapolis: Bobbs-Merrill.

Smith, Adam. [1763] 1956. *Lectures on Justice, Police, Revenue, and Arms*. New York: Kelley & Millman.

_____.[1776] 1976. *An Inquiry into the Nature and Causes of the Wealth of Nations*. Oxford: Clarendon Press.

Smith, Ralph L. 1965. *The Tarnished Badge*. New York: Crowell.

Smith, Rodney T. 1976. "The Legal and Illegal Markets for Taxed Goods: Pure Theory and an Application to State Government Taxation of Distilled Spirits." *Journal of Law and Economics* 19 (August): 393–430.

Stigler, George J. 1971. "The Theory of Economic Regulation." *The Bell Journal of Economics and Management Sciences* 2 (Spring): 3–21.

Stigler, George J., and Gary S. Becker. 1977. "De Gustibus Non Est Disputandum." *American Economic Review* 67(March): 76–90.

Sullivan, Edward D. [1929] 1971. *Rattling the Cup on Chicago Crime*. Freeport, N.Y.: Books for Libraries.

Sumner, Michael T., and Robert Ward. 1981. "Tax Changes and Cigarette Prices." *Journal of Political Economy* 89, no. 6 (December): 1261–65.

Sylbing, G. 1985. *The Use of Drugs, Alcohol and Tobacco: Results of a Survey among Young People in the Netherlands Aged 15–24 Years*. Amsterdam: Foundation for the Scientific Study of Alcohol and Drug Use.

Sylbing, G. and J. M. G. Persoon. 1985. "Cannabis Use among Youth in the Netherlands." *Bulletin On Narcotics* 37 (October/December): 51–60.

Szasz, Thomas S. 1985. *Ceremonial Chemistry: The Ritual Persecution of Drugs, Addicts, and Pushers.* Rev. ed. Holmes Beach, Fla.: Learning Publications.

———.1987. "The Morality of Drug Control." In *Dealing with Drugs: Consequences of Government Control,* edited by Ronald Hamowy, 327–51. Lexington, Mass.: Lexington Books.

Tagliacozzo, G. 1945. "Croce and the Nature of Economic Science." *Quarterly Journal of Economics* 59 (May): 307–29.

Taylor, Arnold H. 1969. *American Diplomacy and the Narcotics Traffic, 1900–1939: A Study in International Humanitarian Reform.* Durham, N.C.: Duke University Press.

Thornton, Mark. 1983. "The Potency of Marijuana under Prohibition." Manuscript. Auburn, Ala.: Auburn University.

———.1986. "The Potency of Illegal Drugs." Manuscript. Auburn, Ala.: Auburn University.

———.1991A. "Economists on Illegal Drugs." *Atlantic Economic Journal.* June 1991. Forthcoming.

———.1991B. "Alcohol Prohibition Was a Failure." *Policy Analysis.* Washington, D.C.: Cato Institute. Forthcoming.

Timberlake, James H. *Prohibition and the Progressive Movement: 1900–1920.* Cambridge, Mass.: Harvard University Press.

Tollison, Robert D., ed. 1986. *Smoking and Society: Toward a More Balanced Assessment.* Lexington, Mass.: Lexington Books.

Towne, Charles Hanson. 1923. *The Rise and Fall of Prohibition.* New York: Macmillan.

Trebach, Arnold S. 1987. *The Great Drug War: And Radical Proposals That Could Make America Safe Again.* New York: Macmillan.

Tyrrell, Ian R. 1979. *Sobering Up: From Temperance to Prohibition in Antebellum America, 1800–1860.* Westport, Conn.: Greenwood Press.

U.S. Department of Justice. Bureau of Justice Statistics. 1984–89. *Sourcebook of Criminal Justice Statistics.* Washington, D.C.: Government Printing Office.

———. Public Integrity Section, Criminal Division. 1989. "Report to the Congress on the Activities and Operations of the Public Integrity Section." Washington, D.C.: (mimeographed).

U.S. National Commission on Law Observance and Enforcement. 1931. *Enforcement of the Prohibition Laws of the United States.* 71st Cong., 3d sess., House Doc. 722.

U.S. Treasury Department. Special Committee of Investigation. 1919. *Traffic in Narcotic Drugs.* Washington, D.C.: Government Printing Office.

Votey, Harold L., and Llad Phillips. 1976. "Minimizing the Social Cost of Drug Abuse: An Economic Analysis of Alternatives for Policy." *Policy Sciences* 7 (September): 315–36.

Walker, William O., III. 1989. *Drug Control in the Americas.* Rev. ed. Albuquerque: University of New Mexico Press.

Wallace, George B. 1944. *The Marihuana Problem in the City of New York: Sociological, Medical, Psychological Studies.* Lancaster, Penn.: Jaques Cattell Press.

Walton, Robert P. 1938. *Marijuana: America's New Drug Problem.* Philadelphia: Lippincott.

Warburton, Clark. 1932. *The Economic Results of Prohibition.* New York: Columbia University Press.

_____.1934. "Prohibition." *Encyclopaedia of the Social Sciences.* Edited by Edwin R. A. Seligman. Vol. 12. London: Macmillan.

Weeden, William B. [1890] 1963. *Economic and Social History of New England: 1620–1789.* 2 vols. New York: Hillary House.

The White House Office of Policy Development. Drug Abuse Policy Office. 1985. *1984 National Strategy: For Prevention of Drug Abuse and Drug Trafficking.* Washington, D.C.: Government Printing Office.

Wickersham Report. See U.S. National Commission on Law Observance and Enforcement.

Williams, Robert H. 1973. *Vice Squad.* New York: Crowell.

Wilson, James Q., and Richard J. Herrnstein. 1985. *Crime and Human Nature: The Definitive Study of the Causes of Crime.* New York: Simon and Schuster.

Wooddy, Carroll H. 1934. *The Growth of the Federal Government, 1915–1932.* New York: McGraw-Hill.

Index

ABC News poll, 76n
Abel, C. T., 107
Abel, Ernest L., 65
abolitionist movement, 43, 46, 48
absenteeism of employees, impact of
alcohol consumption on, 25–27,
26 (table), 28–29, 29 (table)
abstinence pledges, 44–45
addiction: and criminal risk-taking
with price changes, 117, 119 (fig.),
119–20; and deterrent effect of
punishment, 31; discovery of, 4,
58–59; and elasticity of demand
with price changes, 117, 118 (figs.);
extent of, 60n; and individual
rationality, 10, 31, 35–38;
infeasibility of prohibition as
deterrent to, 144; and maintenance
programs, 33, 34n, 64, 147–48; to
patent medicines, 61, 141; and
potency, 91; rehabilitation of, 31n,
33; as side-effect of war, 5, 57, 62,
64–65; solutions to, 152; utility of,
35–36, 37, 38
ad valorem tax: effect on product
attributes, 93–95; prohibition as,
97, 98–99
advertising, and market information,
78, 151
Afghanistan, 136n
Alchian, Armen A., 93, 94 (table)

alcohol: association of use with
criminal behavior, 111, 115,
124–25; consumption patterns,
13–14, 20–21, 28, 29, 101–3, 103
(table), 104 (table), 124–25, 126,
145n; definition as poison, 52n;
economic losses, 23–29; "grip,"
17–18; health risks, 73n, 104–5;
home production, 21; increased
potency under prohibition, 89, 90,
103–5; medicinal use, 52n;
"normal use," 18; potency absent
prohibition, 91; regulation of
markets, 40, 41–43, 51, 54–55, 69,
121–22, 140, 149; substitutes,
20–21, 28, 57–58, 60, 61n, 67;
substitution for other drugs,
144n.3; utility of consumption, 36
alcohol, prohibition of, 86;
association with crime and
corruption, 112, 122–24, 126, 127,
133–35; changes in relative prices,
101–2, 102 (table); contemporary
efforts to reintroduce, 39; costs,
23, 25, 27, 29, 100 (table),
100–101; creation of profit
opportunities, 117, 123; demand
relative to price differences, 102–3,
103 (table); discussion in
economics texts, 10; dismissal of
honest agents, 81–82; economists

167